KT-214-327

£1·20p.

BOUGAINVILLE

ABOUT THE BOOK

"To English-speaking people, the name
Bougainville is immediately associated
with the lovely thorny climbing plant
known as Bougainvilia, and it is to
Bougainville that its discovery and
importation into Europe and America
is attributed. The assumption follows
that he was a botanist, but in fact he was
no more a botanist than was that other
great circumnavigator of the world,
Captain James Cook. Bougainville was
a man of many parts, a man who in
the Italian Rennaissance might have
qualified as a *uomo universale*. The fame,
however, of his journey round the world,
and particularly of his visit to Tahiti,
has almost entirely eclipsed the other
brilliant exploits of this truly remarkable
man."

So begins Michael Ross's captivating
narrative of the life of this fascinating
and versatile man, who confronted
George Washington at Fort Necessity,
and captained a ship at the Battle of
Chesapeake Bay in the American
Revolution, was aide-de-camp to
Montcalm during the Anglo-Canadian
wars, wrote a treatise on integral calculus
at the age of twenty-four, and led one
of the most exciting and valuable
expeditions around the world.

ABOUT THE AUTHOR

Michael Ross was born in 1905 and
has led an active career as an artist, writer
and broadcaster. Among his previous
books are *People of the Mirage*, about his
own trek across the Sahara; *The Reluctant
King*, praised by the *New Yorker* as a
"lucid biography" of Joseph Bonaparte;
The Banners of the King; and recently
Cross the Great Desert, about the life of
René Caillié. His paintings are included
in many distinguished collections,
including the National Gallery of Canada
and the National Maritime Museum of
Richmond, Virginia, and the British Arts
Collection.

Michael R.

BOUGAINVILLE

by Michael Ross

With drawings by the author

Gordon & Cremonesi

© Michael Ross, 1978

All rights reserved. No part of this publication
may be reproduced, stored in a retrieval system, or
transmitted in any form or by any means, electronic,
mechanical, photocopying, recording or otherwise,
without permission in writing from the publishers.

Designed by Heather Gordon
Set in 11 on 13 pt Bembo and printed in Great Britain by
The Anchor Press Ltd and bound by Wm Brendon & Son Ltd
both of Tiptree, Essex

British Library Cataloguing in Publication Data

Ross, Michael, b. 1905
    Bougainville.
    1. Bougainville, Louis Antoine de   2. Explorers,
French – Biography
    910.'92'4   G256.B6   77–30500

LCCN 77–030500
ISBN 0–86033–059–1

Gordon & Cremonesi Publishers
London and New York
New River House
34 Seymour Road
London N8 0BE

Contents

BOOK ONE

MATHEMATICIAN AND SOLDIER

Breadfruit, introduced and acclimatized to the
Island of Reunion by Commerson. Banks discovered
it a year later on Captain Cook's expedition.

Nassauria, found by Commerson in the Straits of
Magellan and named in honour of the young Prince
of Siegen-Nassau.

Chapter One

Youth—Election to the Royal Society of London— Beginning of the Canadian War

To English-speaking people, the name Bougainville is immediately associated with the lovely climbing plant known as Bougainvilia, and it is to Bougainville that its discovery and importation into Europe and America is attributed. The assumption follows that he was a botanist, but in fact he was no more a botanist than was that other great circumnavigator of the world, Captain James Cook. Bougainville was a man of many parts, a man who in Italian Renaissance times might have qualified as a *uomo universale* (universal man). The fame, however, of his journey round the world, and particularly of his visit to Tahiti, has almost entirely eclipsed the other brilliant exploits of this truly remarkable man.

Louis-Antoine de Bougainville was the youngest of four children born to Maître Pierre-Yves de Bougainville and Marie-Françoise d'Arboulin. His birth certificate records that he was born in Paris on 12 November 1729 in the rue Barre du Bec (since renamed rue du Temple). Despite the "de" before his name, he was, as the French say, of "no particular birth". His father, who had pretensions to be descended from the Sieurs de Bougainville, a noble family from Picardy, now long since defunct, was a notary of the Châtelet (the Paris Courts of Justice), his grandfather and uncle were also members of the justiciary, as was his brother, Jean-Pierre, seven years his senior, a brilliant classical scholar and member of the Académie des Inscriptions and Académie Française.

Louis-Antoine's mother, who died when he was still an infant, was also of the *haute bourgeoisie*; her brother, Jean Potentien d'Arboulin, was Directeur des Postes de l'Orléanais, a man of substance, and a close friend of Madame de Pompadour, who familiarly referred to him as "Boubou". "Boubou" was devoted to his nephews and was to be largely instrumental in furthering Louis-Antoine's future career. On his mother's death, he was, to all intents, adopted by the charming and attractive widow of M. Hérault, a former Lieutenant de Police[1]—an office which, despite what sounds to English ears a humble title, ranked among the most important in the magistrature. On his retirement M. Hérault was succeeded by his son and later by his son-in-law by a former marriage. Mme Hérault herself was the daughter of the Contrôleur Général des

Finances, Moreau de Séchelles, while her brother-in-law, M. de Moras, was to
become Minister of the Marine during Bougainville's service in Canada. Therefore, although of "no particular birth", young Bougainville certainly had
extremely useful connections. Mme Hérault, whom Bougainville was always
to address as *chère maman* in his very extensive correspondence with her, was to
prove a real mother to him and in later years was to use in his support her very
considerable influence in social and political circles. Her house was a real home
for him, and her own son, always referred to as Hérault, *tout court*—or, affection-
ately, in the family circle, as Monsieur Bonhomme—was Bougainville's closest
companion until separated from him by war and then his death, at the Battle of
Minden (1759).

Little is recorded of Bougainville's early childhood, but we do know that
he was devoted to his elder brother and always hoped that one day he too might
achieve academic honours. We also know that d'Alembert, the mathematician
and *encyclopédiste*, and Alexis Clairaut, the precocious author of *La Théorie de
la figure de la terre*, were neighbours of Maître de Bougainville and that both took
a lively interest in the boy's education, an interest which was well repaid. It was
Maître de Bougainville's wish that Louise-Antoine should follow in his footsteps and become a lawyer. Dutifully, Louis-Antoine attended the University
of Paris, where, apart from his law studies, he acquitted himself exceptionally
well as a classical scholar and linguist, and, above all, as a mathematician. Young
Bougainville, however, was by no means a pedant. He was "a true Parisian"—
that is to say, he indulged in the pleasures of the town just like any other young
man of the period. He enjoyed a game of cards and female society and developed
a passion for fencing. He was a regular attendant at a fashionable fencing academy,
run by a retired officer of *mousquetaires*, where, after dining, the room was cleared
and foils were produced and the real business of the evening began. There he
crossed swords with such fashionable gentlemen as the Marquis de Saint-Marc,
the Comte de Lameth, the Chevalier de Chastellux, the old Comte de Coulain-
court and the Marquis de la Grange. He also attended a riding academy, for he
was to prove himself an able horseman.

It is difficult to see in the portraits of him Bougainville the young man about
town, the expert swordsman, and the scholar engaged on the first volume of his
*Traité de calcul intégral, pour servir de suite à l'analyse des infiniments petits de
Monsieur le Marquis de l'Hôpital*, which he was to dedicate to the Comte
d'Argenson, Secretary of War. His portraits show him as a plump, jolly fellow,
far removed from the conventional idea of a young blade, a scholar, or the
heroic soldier and mariner which he was to prove himself to be.

That he was called to the bar is certain, but whether he ever practised has
been a matter of speculation. If he did, it was not for long. He probably found
the dry-as-dust atmosphere of a lawyer's office uncongenial to his restless spirit,
for we next find him commissioned *aide-major* in the Picardy militia and a short
while later as a lieutenant of the *mousquetaires noirs*, one of two élite regiments

under the patronage of the King.[2] He was almost immediately appointed aide-de-camp to General Chevert, one of the most distinguished generals of the late War of the Austrian Succession. In this same year, the first volume of young Bougainville's *Traité de calcul intégral* was published (1755) and received instant recognition in academic circles.

He had scarcely spent a year in the service of Chevert when he was appointed third secretary to the Marquis (later Duc) de Mirepoix's embassy to the Court of St James's in London. Chevert, although sorry to lose him, had highly recommended Bougainville for the post. Probably d'Argenson, who knew Mirepoix well and was flattered by the fact that Bougainville had dedicated his treatise to him, had also recommended him for the appointment. No doubt his uncle d'Arbouville also put in a good word on his behalf.

De Mirepoix's mission in London was a delicate one, and it was unfortunate that this excellent soldier was an extremely inept diplomat. Though it had brought to an end the War of the Austrian Succession, the Treaty of Aix-la-Chapelle (1748) had achieved practically nothing else. Diplomatic relations between France and Britain still remained strained. Clive and Dupleix in India were still openly at war, while in North America the vexed question of Anglo-French boundaries had remained unresolved. It should be remembered that the French claimed all the territory between the Alleghenies and the Rockies, from Mexico and Florida to the North Pole, with the exception of the ill-defined British trading posts bordering Hudson Bay. To these vast regions, with adjacent islands, the French had given the name of New France. They controlled the highways to the north, for they had seized the St Lawrence and ensconced themselves at the mouth of the Mississippi. Canada in the north and Louisiana in the south were the keys to the interior, still unexploited and rich with incalculable possibilities. The British colonies, shut in as they were between the Atlantic Ocean and the Allegheny Mountains and Appalachian Highlands, had no royal road to the great interior.

In 1749 the French were becoming increasingly alarmed by the encroachments of British settlers westward. Orders were therefore sent to Admiral de La Galisonnière, Governor of Canada, to build forts on the Ohio, "but only such as were absolutely necessary", for it was the Ohio basin which was the most vulnerable. Further British infiltration was to be prevented, but this was to be done "with the greatest politeness and to give no rise to a *casus belli*". Traders in furs, the staple commodity, were welcome, but not settlers. But what could be more natural than that the British colonists, hemmed in between mountains and sea, should wish to expand? Owing to the stupidity of French policy in denying Protestants the right to emigrate, the vast lands which lay beyond the British colonies remained only a broad tract of wilderness, primeval forest, interspersed with innumerable streams, lakes and craggy mountains, ranged by savage Indians. In 1750 these lands were still a howling waste, yielding nothing to civilization but beaver skins, with here and there a trading post, and on the

Mississippi and Detroit one or two small hamlets. The colonies of New England refused to acknowledge the French boundaries, and both sides courted the Indian tribes to harass their rivals. In 1754, however, there occurred an event which, small though it was, was to lead to war. A small stockaded blockhouse originally built by the British and strategically situated on the forks of the Ohio, where the rivers Monagahela and Allegheny meet to form La Belle Rivière, and where Pittsburgh stands today, was captured by a force of French and their Indian allies and renamed Fort Duquesne. The importance of this site lay in the fact that it was regarded as one of the principal keys to the West. Robert Dinwiddie, Lieutenant-Governor of Virginia, was determined to recover this small but all-important stronghold.

Colonel George Washington, a young officer of the Virginia militia, with a detachment of 159 men, exclusive of Indian allies, was entrusted with the task. From the outset the expedition seemed to be ill-starred. Horsedrawn wagons were to drag the soldiers' meagre supplies over rugged mountains; Washington and his small force were obliged to hew their way through dense forests. When, on 24 May 1754, the column at last reached the Great Meadows, a wide clearing intersected by brooks, and an admirable site on which to establish a base, many of Washington's Virginians were without shoes or stockings, some without shirts. Here, within a few miles of Fort Duquesne, Washington built a small stockaded blockhouse, which he named Fort Necessity.

Three days later Indian scouts brought news that a body of French soldiers lay hidden in a ravine five miles to the west. From their covert actions, Washington anticipated an attack on his small force. After posting a strong guard over his stores and ammunition he headed west to seek them out. Two Indian braves scouted ahead. They returned with news that some thirty French and Indians were in a very obscure rocky glen only about half a mile off the trail.

Washington decided to surround them. The French were taken completely by surprise. Within fifteen minutes after the first shot was fired, the French had surrendered. Ten men had been killed, including the ensign in command, Coulon de Jumonville; the remainder were taken prisoner. The French captives protested that they had had no hostile intentions and were merely on their way to deliver a message from Contrecoeur, the Commandant of Fort Duquesne, demanding that the British should withdraw to the east of the Alleghenies. Washington did not believe this for a moment; nor, for that matter, did anyone else present. The French even went so far as to claim that at the time he was shot, Jumonville, under a flag of truce, was already beginning to parley. This was palpably untrue, and not even credited in French official circles. One thing was certain: the French would retaliate in force. Washington therefore fell back on Fort Necessity. Sure enough, at dawn on 3 July the French, commanded by Villiers de Jumonville, brother of the dead ensign, and with 900 men and a swarm of Indians, attacked. The fight lasted nearly nine hours, in driving rain. At eight o'clock in the evening the French called out, "Voulez-vous parler?"

Washington hesitated, but finally agreed to send two of his men who had some knowledge of French to discuss terms of capitulation. Indeed, he had little alternative: a third of his force had been killed or wounded, all the transport animals and livestock had been shot dead, and some of his men had broken into the rum kegs and were drunk.

After a long absence, his envoys returned with the articles of surrender for Washington's signature: Villiers wanted it on record that, since no state of war had officially been declared, his brother's death should be regarded as murder. Unfortunately, one of Washington's envoys, a Dutchman, whose French was by no means perfect, had mistranslated the words "l'assassinat du Sieur de Jumonville" as "the *death* of the Sieur de Jumonville". To Washington the terms seemed generous. It was useless for him to expose his men to further loss of life and suffering. He therefore agreed to an honourable capitulation, little realizing that he had admitted to murder. Early in the morning of 4 July—a date twice memorable in American history—Fort Necessity was abandoned, and, with drums beating and flag flying, the British force, without transport and with the sound carrying the wounded on their backs, set out on its long, nightmare trek over the mountains back to its base at Albany.

When the news of Jumonville's "murder" reached France, there was an outcry of real or assumed horror. In Europe, Washington was to be held responsible for starting the Seven Years War. Horace Walpole, using words almost identical to those of Voltaire, declared, "A volley fired by a young Virginian in the backwoods of America set the world on fire."

Although the "murder" of Jumonville could be regarded as a *casus belli*, it was in the interest of France to put off an official rupture and pose in an attitude of good faith, while increasing her American garrisons and seeking to prevent further encroachments by the British. The British, however, were not prepared to sit still and wait. Two regiments, each of 500 men, were ordered to set sail for Virginia, where their number was to be raised by local enlistment to 700 apiece. Major-General Edward Braddock was appointed to the command.

No sooner was this development known in Versailles than a French counter-expedition was prepared, on a larger scale. Eighteen ships of war were fitted out for sea at Brest and Rochefort, and 3,000 men were ordered on board. Baron Dieskau, a German veteran who had served under Marshal Saxe in the late War of the Austrian Succession, was appointed Commander-in-Chief; with him went the Canadian-born Marquis de Vaudreuil, to succeed Duquesne as Governor of Canada.

During these preparations there was a great deal of diplomatic correspondence between Versailles and the Court of St James's. De Mirepoix demanded to know why British troops were sent to America. In reply, Sir Thomas Robinson, Secretary of State for the Colonies, answered evasively that there was no intention of disturbing the peace; but the secret orders given to Braddock were far from pacific. Robinson, in turn, demanded of de Mirepoix the purpose of the French armament at Brest and Rochefort. The reply, like that of the British, was that no hostilities were intended, despite the fact that secret orders were sent to Governor Duquesne to attack and destroy Fort Halifax, the key point for a possible British advance on Quebec. But, in making the attack (which in fact never took place), Duquesne was expressly enjoined to pretend that he was acting without orders. Thus there was no good faith on either side. Perhaps the most blatant lack of it was shown by the British.

Not only had the British Government known perfectly well of the French naval and military preparations, but, in addition, it had even known the proposed date of departure of the French fleet (April–May 1755). Admirals Boscawen and Holbourne were ordered to capture or destroy any vessels bound for America. Boscawen, who got to sea before the French, stationed himself off the southern coast of Newfoundland to intercept La Motte, the French admiral; but, with the exception of three ships, the French squadron managed to elude him and complete its journey, some vessels proceeding to Louisbourg, others to Quebec. The three French ships that became separated from the main squadron had become lost in fog and rain, tossing on an angry sea off Cape Race. One of them was the *Alcide*, commanded by a Captain Hocquart, to whom we owe our account of what happened. The wind fell, he tells us, but the fogs continued at intervals until the afternoon of 7 June, when, the weather having cleared, the watch on the maintop saw the distant ocean studded with ships. It was the fleet of Boscawen. On the following morning, the British were about three leagues distant from the French, crowding all sail in pursuit. Towards eleven o'clock, one of the British ships, the *Dunkirk*, was abreast of the *Alcide* to windward, within hailing distance. Hocquart called out, "Are we at peace or war?" He declares that Howe, captain of the *Dunkirk*, replied in French, "La paix, la paix." Hocquart then asked the name of the British admiral, and hearing it was Boscawen replied, "I know him; he is a friend of mine." Being asked his own name, he affirms that he scarcely had time to reply before the guns of the *Dunkirk* opened a devastating fire on the crowded decks of the *Alcide*. She returned the fire, but was soon forced to strike her colours. At the same time one of the other ships, the *Lis*, was attacked and overpowered. The French casualties were heavy, and eight companies of infantry were captured. The third French ship escaped under cover of fog.

This incident, though less well known than the so-called "murder" of Jumonville (probably because it redounds to the discredit of the Royal Navy), brought an end to negotiations on Tuesday, 22 July 1755. In the words of Francis Parkman, "the sword was drawn and brandished in the face of Europe". De Mirepoix and his embassy, including Bougainville, were recalled to France, but it was not until a year later that war was "officially" declared.

Bougainville's appointment to London had lasted less than a year, but for the young soldier–diplomat this period had by no means been wasted. Despite the strained relations between France and Britain, Bougainville made many friends in London and regularly attended meetings of the Royal Society, where, as the author of the *Traité de calcul intégral*, a work which was already well known to many of the Society's members, he was always welcome. Naturally, his official duties had made him familiar with the details of the situation in America, and he had made a careful study of the geography of Canada, the Great Lakes and Ohio valley. Although enjoying the social life of Georgian England (his biographer Maurice Thiéry hints that he had several love affairs there) he still found time to work on the second volume of his treatise and perfect his knowledge of the English language.

Immediately upon his return to France he rejoined his regiment and resumed his appointment as aide-de-camp to Chevert. The regiment was stationed at Richemont, on the Moselle between Metz and Thionville. The war clouds were already gathering over Europe and the French army on the Rhine was on a war footing. At Richemont he was joined by young Hérault. It was his mother (according to René de Kérallain) who had arranged for him to join Bougainville there, "in the hopes that each would help to restrain the rash conduct of the other"—an enlightening comment on one side of Bougainville's character. It is unlikely, however, that either young man had time or opportunity to indulge in frivolity. Chevert was a stern disciplinarian. Leave, even compassionate leave, was seldom granted; hunting was strictly forbidden. A company of players came from Metz from time to time to entertain the troops; other amusements— jugglers, clowns and so on—were provided by the officers at their own expense. Officers were obliged to engage in arms drill and in other military activities such as private soldiers had to perform. (This discipline had always applied to the *mousquetaires*, nearly all of whom were recruited from the impoverished *petite noblesse* of Gascony and Béarn.)

Bougainville earned the highest praise from Chevert. In a letter to d'Argenson he signalized both young Hérault and Bougainville for their dedication to duty. It was while Bougainville was in Richemont that he received the wonderful news that he had been elected a Fellow of the Royal Society of London. For a twenty-seven-year-old French officer, whose country was in all but name at war with Britain, this was indeed an honour. In the meanwhile he was preparing for the press the second volume of his *Traité de calcul intégral*.

Chapter Two

Aide-de-Camp to Montcalm

While Bougainville was in Richemont, the situation in America had, with the arrival of Braddock and his two regiments of regular infantry, and of the French reinforcements under Dieskau, become much more serious. Even before the arrival of Braddock, Shirley, the energetic sixty-year-old Governor of Massachusetts, had been drawing up plans for a four-pronged attack on the French. Braddock was to drive the French out of Fort Duquesne and thus secure the Ohio basin; Shirley himself was to reduce Fort Niagara, which barred the entrance to Lake Ontario; a force of provincials, under the command of the Irish colonel William Johnson (who had great influence over the Indians), was to reduce Crown Point, which guarded access to Lake Champlain, one of the watery highways leading to Quebec; and Colonel Monckton, a regular officer of great distinction, was to capture Fort Beauséjour, on the Bay of Fundy, and thus bring Acadia (Nova Scotia) into complete subjection. It was a plan which met with the entire approval of the British Government; indeed, it was a plan which had already been conceived in the minds of the Premier, the Duke of Newcastle, and of the Duke of Cumberland, Commander-in-Chief of the British army. To strike this fourfold blow in time of peace was worthy of the thoroughly inept Newcastle and the bull-headed royal Duke. The pretext was that the positions to be attacked were all on British soil; that in occupying them the French had been guilty of invasion; and that to expel the invaders was an act of self-defence. Yet, with regard to two of the positions, the French, if they had no other right, might at least claim one of prescription. Crown Point had been undisturbed in their possession for twenty-four years, and Niagara, which New York claimed, but from which it had not been attempted to dislodge the French, had first been occupied by them three-quarters of a century before.

Unfortunately, owing to lack of support from those British provincial governors not immediately threatened by French encroachment, all the British plans, with one exception, went awry. It was therefore only after many delays that Braddock, short of supplies, short of transport—indeed, short of every-thing—set out for Fort Duquesne, with George Washington as aide-de-camp. Braddock, a brave but obstinate, narrow-minded general, refused to accept Washington's advice or that of other provincial officers accustomed to Indian and Canadian warfare. Thus, when eventually the British redcoats, drilled to fight on European soil, found themselves confronted by the howling Indians and almose equally savage Canadian rangers who constituted the garrison of Fort Duquesne, they were at a complete disadvantage. As they advanced through dense forest, the illusive enemy, darting behind trees, selected his individual target. In brief, the British force was utterly routed. Of the 2,000 who started out on that fatal day of 8 July 1755, only 977 returned. Braddock himself was mortally wounded.

Shirley, for his part, never reached Fort Niagara. Bedevilled, as usual, by lack of provisions and transport, and also by fever, and having to force their way through swamp and forest, dragging on sleds over ground strewn with rocks and fallen trees the *bateaux* (flat-bottomed craft) by which they had ascended the Mohawk, it is a wonder that they got as far as "the miserable little fort of Oswego" on the shores of Lake Ontario. On arrival there, only about 1,500 men were fit for duty. Fifty miles northwards, across the lake, lay the French Fort Frontenac, strongly garrisoned. Without first reducing this stronghold, any further advance was out of the question. The French, who were well equipped with vessels, even armed sloops, were ready, so soon as Shirley should make a move, to swoop down on Oswego and cut off his communications with his base. The situation was hopeless. After calling a meeting of his officers, Shirley decided to return home by the way he had come, leaving just a small holding force behind.

Johnson was more successful, although he never achieved his objective of reaching Crown Point. Dieskau, personally in command of the French troops, advanced south down Lake Champlain to meet him on the shores of Lake Sacrament (today Lake George). In a furious battle, during which the advantage swung back and forth, from one side to the other, the French eventually were defeated and Dieskau, severely wounded three times, was taken prisoner and eventually removed to England. Johnson, too, had been wounded and took little part in the battle, the successful outcome of which was entirely owing to the heroic example of his second-in-command, Phineas Lyman, a lawyer from Connecticut. It was Johnson, however, who was treated as the hero of the day: the British Government awarded him £5,000 and created him a baronet. But Crown Point remained in French hands.

The only truly successful British operation in this campaign, which did little more than exacerbate French feelings, was the capture of Fort Beauséjour by Monckton, and the subsequent reduction of other French strongpoints along the shores of the Bay of Fundy. But of the fate of the Acadians, who had been British subjects for forty years—ever since the signing of the Treaty of Utrecht —more will be said later, since their lot was to affect profoundly the whole of Bougainville's future.

On 18 May 1756, Britain, after a year of open hostility to France, finally declared war. To quote Francis Parkman,

> She had attacked France by land and sea, turned loose her ships to prey upon French commerce, and brought some three hundred prizes into her ports. It was the act of a weak Government supplying by spasms of violence what it lacked in considerate resolution. France, no match for her amphibious enemy in the game of marine depredation, cried out in horror. . . . On 9 June, she too declared war and now began the most terrible conflict of the eighteenth century; one that convulsed Europe and shook America, India, the coasts of Africa, and the islands of the sea. (*Montcalm and Wolfe*, vol. I.)

It is no part of our story to describe in detail the causes of the Seven Years War, but for readers unfamiliar with the circumstances a very short outline may not be out of place. The existing tangle of smothered discords, ambitions, treaties between rival European powers, and offensive and defensive alliances was such that a blow at one point was bound to shake the whole fabric. Francis Parkman explains,

> Hanover, like the heel of Achilles, was the vulnerable part for which England was always trembling. Therefore she made a defensive treaty with Prussia, by which each party bound itself to aid the other, should its territory be invaded. England thus sought a guaranty against France, and Prussia against Russia. . . . Prussia's King, Frederick the Great, had drawn upon himself an avalanche. Three women—two empresses and a concubine—controlled the forces of the three great nations, Austria, Russia and France; and they all hated him: Elizabeth of Russia, by reason of distrust fomented by secret intrigue and turned into gall by the biting tongue of Frederick himself . . . who had compared her to Messalina . . . ; Maria Theresa of Austria because she saw in him a rebellious vassal of the Holy Roman Empire, and above all because he had robbed her of Silesia; Madame de Pompadour, because when she sent him a message of compliment, he had answered, "Je ne la connais pas" ["I don't know her"], and forbade his ambassador to visit her, and because his mocking wit spared neither her nor her royal lover. Feminine pique, revenge or vanity had then at their service the mightiest armaments in Europe. . . .
>
> The recovery of Silesia and the punishment of Frederick for seizing it, possessed the mind of Maria Theresa with the force of a ruling passion. To these ends she had joined herself in secret league with Russia, and now at the prompting of her minister Kaunitz, courted the alliance with France, thus reversing Austria's hereditary policy by

joining hands with her old and deadly foe, and spurning England, of late her most trusted ally.

But France could give powerful aid against Frederick, and hence the high-born, virtuous and proud Maria Theresa stooped to make advances to the all-powerful mistress of Louis XV, even addressing her as "Ma chère cousine". Mme de Pompadour was delighted and could hardly do enough for her imperial friend. Was she not all powerful? She ruled the King and could make and unmake ministers at will; they hastened to do her pleasure, disguising their sycophancy and subservience to her wishes as "reasons of state". (Ibid.)

Henceforth France was to turn her strength against her European foes, committing over 100,000 men to the field. The American war was to hold second place in the eyes of the King's omnipotent mistress. Still, something had to be done to replace Dieskau, who had been taken to England. None of the Court favourites wanted a command in the backwoods of Canada. D'Argenson could choose whom he would. His choice fell on Louis-Joseph, Marquis de Montcalm-Gozon de Saint Véran, a soldier who had distinguished himself in the Thirty Years War.

Montcalm had much in common with Bougainville. As a young boy Montcalm had written to his father what he considered his aims should be:

First, to be an honourable man of good morals, brave and a Christian. Secondly, to read in moderation; to know as much of French and Latin as most men of the world; also the four rules of arithmetic, and something of history, geography and French and Latin *belles lettres*, as well as to have a taste for the arts and sciences. Thirdly, and above all, to be obedient . . . to your orders and my dear mother. Fourthly, to fence and ride as well as my small abilities will permit.

In later years he far surpassed these modest aspirations and had ambitions to be elected one day to the Académie. Montcalm and his young aide-de-camp were ideally suited.

With hindsight it is easy to criticize Madame de Pompadour's policies, but what was Bougainville's opinion of the favourite? His brother was a "queen's man", but his uncle Boubou was the friend of the royal mistress and had known her when she was still plain Jeanne Poisson. Whatever he might have thought of the rights or wrongs of the war in Europe for which she was so largely responsible, he certainly had no doubts that the war in America was fully justified. Britain had inexcusably interfered with French commerce and shipping and had launched attacks on French strongholds with intent to expand her own colonial territories. When war broke out, he had had no hesitation in offering his services to France in the cause of preserving her American possessions. While his best friend, Hérault de Séchelles, joined the armies engaged in Germany, Bougainville solicited his uncle Boubou, to obtain for him the post of aide-de-camp to the newly appointed Marquis de Montcalm.

Bougainville's reputation had already preceded him. The Marquise de Pompadour, at Boubou's request, had no hesitation in recommending his appointment; Chevert, too, highly commended him. His appointment therefore was a mere formality.

The elegant Chevalier de Lévis, afterwards Marshal of France, was named as Montcalm's second-in-command, with the rank of brigadier, and the Chevalier de Bourlamaque as third, with the rank of colonel.

It is clear that Bougainville soon earned his new chief's approval, for as early as a month before his departure for Canada Montcalm wrote to his mother, in the peculiar, elliptical, scarcely translatable style typical of all his personal correspondence, "Tomorrow I go to Versailles till Sunday—will write from there to Madame de Montcalm [his wife]—I have three aides-de-camp—one of them Bougainville—man of parts—pleasant company."

By 26 March, Montcalm, with all his following (including Rigaud de Vaudreuil—brother of the Canadian Governor—who, taken prisoner by the British, had escaped to France "by a ruse"), was ready to embark at Brest. Three ships of the line, the *Léopard*, the *Héros* and the *Illustre* were ready to receive the troops, while Montcalm, with de Lévis and de Bourlamaque, were to take passage in the frigates *Licorne*, *Sauvage* and *Sirène*. "I like the Chevalier de Lévis", wrote Montcalm to his mother, "and I think he likes me, but my first aide-de-camp, Bougainville, pleases me if possible still more".

The troops destined to accompany Montcalm to Canada amounted to only two battalions, 1,200 men in all. Yet la Pompadour sent 10,000 men to fight the battles of Austria. Montcalm's troops marched into Brest in the early morning, breakfasted in the town, and went on board the transports "with incredible gaiety", as Bougainville wrote. "What a nation is ours! Happy is he who commands it worthily!"

It was, however, with mixed feelings that Bougainville left France, as is apparent from the letter he wrote to his brother from Brest on 29 March:

> The news you give me of Mme Hérault's health seems to me very bad. It is very hard to carry away with me such cruel anxiety, knowing that I will be at least five months without news. Speak to her sometimes of me, dear brother, and maintain the friendship which she has been kind enough to bestow on an unhappy child who would never have parted from her had he foreseen how things were to turn out. . . . Alas! if the greatest anxiety did not follow me beyond the seas, I would carry away with me the most agreeable impressions. I am delighted with

my general. He is friendly, witty, frank and open minded. I have every reason to believe that he likes me. He hides nothing from me and pays me the honour of consulting me, an honour I repay by not advising him! He is very keen to put my humble services to use and I am happy enough to oblige. What more can I want? We are at the moment [still] hove-to awaiting a favourable wind. The captain of the *Licorne*, M. le Chevalier de Rigaudière, is very friendly and a most distinguished officer. . . . He has promised to teach me as much about seamanship and navigation as possible during our crossing. . . .

I should be much obliged if, when you send the second part of my *Traité de calcul intégral* to the Royal Society, you would also send a copy to Lord Macclesfield [the President] with one of those letters of eight lines which you know how to write so well. . . . Clairaut . . . could put it into English for you.

I send my father and aunt [his father's sister who brought him up in his infancy] a thousand kind words and tell them to keep well and not to worry about me. . . .

The *Licorne* set sail on 3 April at five o'clock in the afternoon, with the *Héros* as escort. The other ships left a few days later. Bougainville, in another letter to his brother, described the journey:

The first days were admirable, fine skies, calm seas, good wind, which, without being too strong, set us well on our course. We met very few English men o' war and those we did meet gave us no chase. On Wednesday of Holy Week we were by our reckoning off the New-foundland Banks. Here we were greeted by a squall which left us tossing in mountainous seas until Easter Day. We were forced to part with the *Héros*, which being a much larger ship than ours was better equipped to weather wind and waves, while we, under one sail only, with the wind astern, ran for Martinique. We covered eighty-seven leagues in twenty-four hours, surmounting waves higher than our own vessel. . . . At last came Easter Day and with it sunshine and calm seas, the weather as warm as summer. . . . Since then we have had, almost always, favourable winds. We entered Quebec harbour thirty-eight days after our departure [on 12 May], an incredibly short crossing when one considers that we sailed about 400 leagues out of our way and were held up for six days [by ice] nine leagues from Quebec.

From Montcalm's description of the same journey it would seem to have been still more hazardous than this suggests. Not only was the *Licorne* tossed about in mountainous seas, but, in addition she was in constant danger from icebergs when off the Newfoundland Banks.

The *Héros* reached Quebec eight days before the *Licorne*. The other ships also arrived safely.

Bougainville stayed in Quebec as the guest of his cousin M. de Vienne, a government official married to a young Canadian. The city gave the King's officers an enthusiastic welcome. The Commissary-General, M. Bigot, gave a sumptuous banquet in honour of Montcalm and his staff. The food was plentiful and good, accompanied by the best wines of France. Bougainville, writing to his brother, felt obliged to observe that "the profession of commissary [whose work it was to provide for the feeding of others] by no means involved starvation for those who exercised it". Bigot, a great favourite of Governor Vaudreuil, was, as Bougainville was soon to learn, a thorough crook who was making a fortune from peculation. On 22 May, Montcalm set out by coach for Montreal to meet the Governor, while Bougainville followed by canoe—a thrilling experience for the young man.

The pattern of the forthcoming campaign had already been decided upon by Vaudreuil. The first move was to capture Fort Oswego on Lake Ontario. Speed was essential if advantage was to be taken of the summer months.

The new general was not welcome to Vaudreuil, who had hoped to command the troops himself and had represented to the French Court that it was needless and inexpedient to send out a general officer from France. The Court, however, had not accepted his views; hence it was with more curiosity than satisfaction that he greeted the colleague who had been assigned to him. He saw before him a man of small stature, with a lively countenance, a keen eye, and, in moments of animation, rapid vehement talk and nervous gesticulation. Montcalm, we may suppose, regarded the Governor with no less attention.

Pierre-François Rigaud, Marquis de Vaudreuil, was the son of Philippe de Vaudreuil, who had governed Canada early in the eighteenth century; he himself had been Governor of Louisiana. He had not the force of character his position demanded and lacked decision in time of crisis. One of his traits was an extreme egotism which made him take credit for every success and throw on others the blame for every failure. He was a man capable of being led by those who had the skill and temperament for the task, but Montcalm, with his impetuous nature, was not the man. Moreover, the fact that Montcalm had been born in France militated against the possibility of gaining the good graces of the Governor. Vaudreuil, Canadian by birth, loved the colony and its people and distrusted Old France and all that came out of it. Moreover, like the majority of Canadian governors, he had connections with the naval service and addressed his official correspondence to the Minister of Marine, while Montcalm communicated with the Minister of War. His relations with the General were not improved by the fact that Montcalm commanded the regulars from France, whose very presence, in the eyes of Vaudreuil, was an evil, though a necessary one. But the Minister of War had made it clear that he wished Montcalm to take immediate command not only of the troops from France but also of the colonial regulars and militia. An order from the King to this effect was sent to Vaudreuil, with instructions to him to communicate it to Montcalm or withhold it, as he thought fit. Vaudreuil lost no time in replying that the General "ought to concern himself with nothing but the troops from France", and returned the order to the Minister of War. The Governor and the General thus represented the two parties which were soon to divide Canada—that of New France and that of Old. Vaudreuil's relations with Dieskau had been little better. The Chevalier de Lévis and de Bourlamaque were equally irritated by the Governor's attitude, but concealed their feelings better than the volatile Montcalm. The elegant de Lévis, taking care to avoid any too serious ruffling of feelings, always addressed Vaudreuil with an impeturbable calm, not without a shade of impertinence; de Bourlamaque, who in his personal relations with the Governor succeeded better than his two colleagues, nevertheless did not hesitate, in his official correspondence, to criticize him in the most caustic terms. Bougainville, although extremely critical of Vaudreuil, on the whole was sufficiently tactful to avoid the Governor's censure.

There was also antagonism between the forces commanded by the two chiefs. These were of three kinds: the *troupes de terre*, or regulars from France; the *troupes de la marine*, or colonial regulars; and, lastly, the militia. The *troupes de la marine* had for a long time formed the permanent establishment of Canada. Though attached to the naval department, they served on land and were employed as a police force within the limits of the colony, or to garrison posts. These troops were enlisted for the most part in France; but they were encouraged to become settlers in the colony when (or, in time of peace, even before) their term of service had expired. Thus the relations of the *troupes de la marine* with the colony were close.

Of the settlers, all active males between the ages of fifteen and sixty were enrolled in the militia and could be called up at any time on orders from the Governor. They received arms, clothing, equipment and rations from the King, but no pay. Their fighting qualities were much like those of the Indians, whom they rivalled in endurance and in forest warfare. As bush-fighters they were unequalled, but for regular battle on the open field they were of small account. They were at first inclined to despise the regulars for their ignorance of woodcraft, and thought themselves able to defend the colony alone, boasting that one true Canadian was a match for three Englishmen.

To the white fighting force must be added the native redskins, the most reliable of whom were the Mission Indians, who lived within the settled area of Canada. Their Catholicism, however, was only skin deep, and they were to prove on occasion as bloodthirsty and cruel in war as their heathen brothers of the west and north, nearly all of whom, since the defeat of Braddock, were at the call of France. Only some of the Iroquois or Confederation of Nations, who were centred on what is now the State of New York, were more or less loyal to the British, but they proved unreliable allies. When, later, French arms were successful, nearly all the tribes openly declared themselves the friends of France.

Despite their mutual antipathy, the Marquis de Montcalm was greeted by Vaudreuil with the old-world courtesy of one gentleman to another. It was agreed that, while it was Montcalm's duty to command the troops in the field, Vaudreuil, in his capacity as Governor, remained his superior; no military operations were to be conducted without his prior approval. Despite Vaudreuil's glaring faults, he was not altogether a fool. Being Canadian-born, the Canadians loved him; thus, if they knew that the General's orders had been endorsed by the Governor, or, as Vaudreuil liked to make out, had been directly inspired by him (so long as their implementation proved successful), the Canadians would unhesitatingly follow the Frenchman.

For over a year the Governor had been planning the attack on Oswego, an operation which, to begin with, Montcalm regarded as impossibly rash. In the past twelve months the British had greatly strengthened their forces in America. Two regiments, under Generals Abercromby and Webb, had been despatched to New York, as had numerous transports loaded with war material. Lord Loudon, a bluff Scottish soldier, had been appointed Commander-in-Chief. The New England colonies, discouraged by Johnson's failure to capture Crown Point, had taken new heart when they learned that the British Government would grant £115,000 in partial compensation for their former sacrifices and had raised a force of some 16,000 men.

Nevertheless, once the decision to reduce Fort Oswego had been taken, Montcalm set to work with characteristic sureness of judgement and execution. Speed was essential. First, however, it was necessary to make a careful inspection of the other French forts. Montcalm therefore set out with the Chevalier de Lévis for Fort Carillon (Ticonderega), at the southern end of Lake Champlain. They made their way up the river Richelieu by canoe, skirted along the western shore of the lake, inspected Fort Saint Frédéric, and disembarked at Carillon on 3 July. There a Canadian engineer, Lotbinière, was leisurely engaged in perfecting the defences, but Montcalm, as Francis Parkman writes, "at once infected everyone with his southern impetuosity, aroused somnolent energies, established the discipline hitherto lacking, received delegations from Indian tribes with saintly patience, carried out reconnaissances of the country around Lake Saint-Sacrament, and towards the head of Lake Champlain, winning the approval and admiration of all" (Montcalm and Wolfe, vol. I).

Satisfied with the results of his visit, he left more than 2,000 men at Carillon, under de Lévis, who deservedly enjoyed his entire confidence. Then he left for Montreal, where he found Bougainville acting instead of the Commissary-General, André Doreil, while awaiting that official's arrival. This administrative work was not at all to Bougainville's liking and he carried out his duties without enthusiasm. He had come to make war, not to sit at a desk. But Bougainville was not a man to waste his time; he had continued his careful observations and jotted down in his journal everything he saw. On 3 July he records that a party of Indians disembarked at Montreal, bringing with them some British prisoners whom they had captured in a surprise attack on a convoy on its way to revictual Fort Oswego. This was a new sight for Bougainville, who describes as follows the triumphal arrival of this tribe, known as the Wild Oats (a sub-group of the Algonquins):

> They came in five great canoes built of bark, bearing six scalps and bringing several prisoners. On arrival before Montreal, they manoeuvred their canoes abreast, and for some time lay to. Then came their salute—a volley of musket fire accompanied by loud cries, to which the forts replied by firing three salvos of cannon. After that, they came alongside and landed, and proceeded in double file towards the château, carrying before them wands decorated with feathers, the prisoners marching between the two ranks. The latter were not ill treated, as sometimes happens on entering towns or the larger villages. On arrival at M. Vaudreuil's residence, the prisoners seated themselves in a circle on the floor, while an Indian chief made a short speech, which surprised me by its vigour and forcefulness.... The Wild Oats, or Menominees, unlike other tribes, who usually keep part of the booty to themselves, brought to their "father" [Vaudreuil] all the "flesh" [prisoners] they had received. After a while they began to dance round the prisoners in a ring to the sound of a sort of tambourine—a strange spectacle more likely to terrify than amuse, yet nevertheless interesting to a *philosophe* desirous of studying human nature, especially in its most primitive state. These men were naked save for a piece of cloth in front and behind; their faces and bodies were bedaubed with paint; feathers, signs and symbols of war, adorned their heads; in their hands were tomahawks and spears. These Indians are, for the most part, vigorous, tall and handsome men. . . . No one could have a better ear for music than these people. Every movement of their bodies synchronizes perfectly with the rhythm. Their dance is similar to the Pyrrhic dances of ancient Greece. As soon as finished, wine and meat were distributed among them. The prisoners were sent off to prison in charge of a detachment, to prevent them from being bashed on the head by the Algonquins and Iroquois of Le Saut, now gathered in Montreal and in mourning for the loss of their fellow tribesmen.

Montcalm and Bougainville exchanged impressions, agreeing, not without humour and with philosophic resignation, that they would indeed have to adapt themselves to bizarre customs.

On 21 July, Montcalm, accompanied by Bougainville with a large escort, left
Montreal by canoe for Fort Frontenac, where the troops for the attack on Fort
Oswego were to be concentrated. Bougainville never ceased to take notes. He
admired the wooded banks of the St Lawrence, the majestic trees and splendour
of the panorama. "Quel dommage qu'un aussi beau terrain soit sans culture"
("What a pity that such a lovely land should be without culture"), he wrote.

The journey was filled with adventure. They pushed up the dangerous
rapids of the St Lawrence to the mouth of the Oswegatchie, where Ogdensburg
stands today. There stood Fort La Présentation, a strongpoint and settlement
built by the Sulpician Abbé Piquet. Piquet, both soldier and missionary, was a
most remarkable man and had set himself the task of winning over the Iroquois
tribes of the region to the French cause. Bougainville was surprised to see one
of the Indian chiefs dressed from head to foot like a Frenchman. "He seemed",
wrote the young aide-de-camp, "like a savage harlequin in a blond wig and
laced hat, a present from the dauphin." Piquet had chosen the site of La Présentation with great skill, not only from a military point of view, but also because
the rich meadows and forests, and the abundance of fish and game found there,
made it an attractive settlement for the Indians. The nature of the spiritual
instruction bestowed by Father Piquet can be gathered from the words of a
proselyte warrior who declared with enthusiasm that he had learned from the
missionary that the King of France was the eldest son of the wife of Jesus
Christ! The effect was to stimulate his devotion to the great Onontio (King)
beyond the sea, and to the lesser Onontio who represented him in Canada.

Montcalm was greatly impressed by this soldier-priest, who not long since
had, on his own initiative, conducted a military reconnaissance, combined with
his own particular brand of proselytization, on the shores of Lake Ontario. He
had made many "converts", though he complained that the natives, including
women and children, were sometimes too drunk on his liberal gifts of brandy
to be in a state to accept immediate conversion! But it was his detailed information concerning Fort Oswego that was of particular interest to the General.
While at La Présentation, Montcalm held ceremonial meetings with the
Indians, to whom he presented gifts of wine, pigs, vermilion and tobacco and
what Bougainville refers to as *porcelaine*, but which, in fact, consisted of neck-
laces and wands made from coloured snail-shells. After the gifts came the ritual
exchange of wampum belts, strings of beads indicative of friendship and the
promise of collaboration in the forthcoming expedition. To Bougainville's
surprise, women attended these councils. "The gravity with which they attended
the deliberations", he wrote, "deserves to be noted. They have, moreover, the
same standing among the Indians that the matrons of old held among the Gauls
and Germans." Bougainville seems never to forget his classical learning.

From La Présentation Montcalm proceeded to Frontenac, where he had left de Bourlamaque to prepare for the reception of the 3,500 men who were to take part in the attack on Oswego. There again there were ceremonial meetings with the redskins, more gifts and further exchanges of wampum belts. What a joy this journey must have been to the always-inquiring mind of Bougainville.

When Shirley had retired from Oswego he had left behind part of his force, who had orders to strengthen the fort and construct vessels. Little had been done. The main fort (there were three in all) was more of a trading post than a stronghold; it was protected by a wall built of rough stones packed with earth, incapable of standing up to artillery fire. No cannon had been provided on the side now exposed to attack. Two guns had been mounted on the trading house in the centre of the fort; but, as the concussion caused by their firing shook down stones from the wall, they had been removed. The second fort, called Fort Ontario, considered the best, stood on a high plateau to the east, on the right side of the river Oswego where it entered the lake. This fort was in the shape of a star, and was formed of tree-trunks set upright in the ground, hewn flat on two sides and closely fitted together—an excellent defence against musketry, but useless against cannon. On a hill, a quarter of a mile beyond Old Oswego, stood the third fort, an unfinished stockade called New Oswego (Fort George) or, by reason of its worthlessness, Fort Rascal. It had served as a cattle pen, and there were no loopholes in the stockade.

On 29 July, Montcalm sent Bougainville across the lake with a reconnaissance party, to inspect the strength of the fortifications. From what they found they concluded that success was assured. This confirmed what Montcalm had already learnt from Piquet, and from deserters and prisoners, who had declared that the main fort was nothing but a loopholed wall held by 600–700 ill-fed, discontented and mutinous men. Bougainville, who because of his knowledge of English, had been detailed to interview the deserters, was told "that they had been driven to desert by the want of good food, and that within a year 1,200 men had already died of disease".

Montcalm, however, was taking no chances. On 4 August all was ready and the amphibious operation began. He had at his disposal a little above 3,000 men, abundantly supplied with artillery. By 10 August, under cover of darkness, all had arrived within a mile or so of the first fort. Four cannon were planted in battery upon the strand and the men bivouacked beside their boats. So skilful were the assailants and so careless the assailed that the British knew nothing of their danger until the following morning, when a reconnoitring canoe discovered the invaders. Two armed vessels came to cannonade them, but their light guns were no match for the French heavy artillery, and they were forced to keep off. Canadians and Indians kept up a brisk fire from the shelter of the surrounding trees, while the French regulars dug trenches and parallels and a strong abattis within 180 yards of the ramparts. Twenty-two more cannon were brought up. The British garrison of Fort Ontario was made up of only 370 men, including raw recruits. They had eight small cannon and a mortar, with which they kept up a brisk fire, but there was no answering shot from the French trenches; nevertheless, it was certain that once the French artillery came into action, the wooden defences would be splintered to pieces. Colonel Mercer, commandant of Oswego, therefore, thinking it better to lose the fort than both fort and garrison, signalled to his men from across the river to abandon their positions and join him on the other side. The garrison passed over un-molested after firing off all their ammunition or throwing it into a well and spiking their guns.

As soon as darkness set in, Montcalm moved up to the deserted fort. Before daybreak. twenty heavy pieces had been dragged up to the plateau, and nine were already in position. Grape and round-shot were soon sweeping the entrenchment dug by the British as an additional defence, and crashing into the rotten masonry of Oswego.

Early on the same morning, Montcalm ordered a force of Indians and Canadians, under the command of Rigaud, to cross the river above the forts. Bougainville was among their number. Although they passed unopposed, for the British never suspected an attack from this direction, the crossing, without boats, was extremely difficult—for Bougainville, if not for the Canadian rangers and Indians. Though in his journal he mentions this episode in the most casual way, it must have represented a considerable ordeal—especially the need to wade with water swirling up to his neck as he held his musket above his head.

All crossed safely and presently showed themselves at the edge of the woods, yelling and firing their guns, too far away to do much damage, but not too far off further to demoralize an already disheartened garrison. The cannonade from the plateau had already effectively achieved its purpose. Colonel Mercer, the soul of the defence, had been cut in two by a cannonball while directing his gunners. Up to this time the defenders had behaved with quite extraordinary spirit, "but despair now seized them, increased by the screams and entreaties of the women, of whom there were more than a hundred in the place". Lieutenant-Colonel Littlehales, second-in-command to Mercer, had no alternative but to surrender. Bougainville was sent forward to propose terms of capitulation. The terms are recorded, but there is no recorded description of the meeting between the Frenchman and the British officer. Bougainville, who had just swum and forded a river, could hardly have presented a picture of elegance, but one can be certain that he conducted himself with his usual courtesy. The British surren-dered 1,600 prisoners, including sailors, labourers and women. This is the figure given by Vaudreuil and is probably an exaggeration. Similarly, the loss on both sides is variously given. By the most trustworthy accounts, the British casualties did not exceed fifty killed and those of the French were even less. But the British lost over a hundred pieces of light artillery, all their remaining powder, shot and shell, and everything that the French were unable to carry away. Oswego and the other forts were burnt to the ground. Father Piquet, who had joined the expedition, planted among the ruins a tall cross and nearby a pole bearing the arms of France. On the cross, Bougainville himself inscribed the words "In hoc signo vincunt" ("In this sign they conquer"); and on the pole he inscribed, "Manibus date lilia plenis" ("Scatter lilies with generous hands"—*Aeneid* VI, 883). "Perhaps not very appropriate", as he wrote to his brother.

On 27 August, Bougainville set out for Montreal to announce the glorious news that Oswego had been captured and utterly destroyed. The enemy had been pushed back within the limits of its old frontiers, and France, mistress of Lake Ontario, would henceforth need only slender garrisons at Frontenac and Niagara to maintain her connections with the west. Montcalm's, lightning strokes had shaken British confidence and it was with legitimate pride that Bougainville wrote to his brother, "I have tasted the pleasure that a first victory gives."

But the news had preceded him and to his disgust Vaudreuil had already written to the Minister of Marine claiming for himself all credit for planning the operation and that its successful issue was entirely due to his brother Rigaud and the Canadians. The pronouns "I" and "my" recur with monotonous frequency in Vaudreuil's reports. "The measures *I* took assured our victory in spite of opposition", he wrote. "If *I* had been less vigilant and firm, Oswego would still be in the hands of the English. *I* cannot sufficiently congratulate *myself* on the zeal which *my* brother and the Canadians and Indians showed on this occasion; for without them, *my* orders would have been given in vain."

What he has to say of the regular officers from France is so defamatory that it probably produced quite the contrary effect to that which he intended. Among the many libellous accusations he makes against them was that they made

> a profit out of their provisions, by having certificates made under borrowed names, so they can draw cash for them on return from the Oswego campaign. It is the same with the soldiers, who also sell their provisions to the King and get paid for them. In conjunction with M. Bigot, I labour to remedy all these abuses and the rules we have established have saved the King a considerable expense. M. de Montcalm has complained very much of these rules.

The Intendant Bigot, who appears here as a reformer, was in fact the centre of a monstrous system of public fraud and malversation.

Examples of Vaudreuil's calumnies, then and later, are too numerous to relate in detail, but one more example is worth recording. He accuses Montcalm and his staff of so antagonizing the Canadians and Indian tribes that they had threatened never to fight again for the French unless under the command of either Vaudreuil himself or his brother Rigaud. The absurdity of this claim will soon become apparent. The face, however, which Vaudreuil turned to Montcalm betrayed nothing of these slanders and it was some time before the General was fully aware to what lengths the Governor had gone to denigrate him in the eyes of the French Court. In his report to the Minister of War, Montcalm wrote, after mentioning the fact that he had occasion to punish some of the Canadians at Oswego, "I must do Monsieur de Vaudreuil the justice to say he approved of my proceedings." He then continues,

> He is a good natured man, mild, with no character of his own, surrounded by people who try to destroy all his confidence in the general of the troops of France. I am praised excessively, in order to make him jealous, excite his Canadian prejudices and prevent him from dealing with me frankly, or adopting my views when he can help it.

Later, Montcalm writes, "I have gained the utmost confidence of the Canadians and Indians: and in the eyes of the former, when I travel or visit their camps, I have the air of a tribune of the people." And in another letter: "The Indians are delighted with me; the Canadians are pleased with me; their officers fear and esteem me. . . ."

In his Journal Bougainville writes of Vaudreuil, drawing as usual on parallels from his beloved classical authors:

> One must be blind not to see that we the French regular forces are treated as the Spartans treated the Helots. The Marquis de Montcalm has not the honour of being consulted and it is generally through public rumour that he first hears of M. de Vaudreuil's military plans. . . . The Governor is a timid man, who can neither make a resolution nor keep one. . . . When V. produces an idea, he falls in love with it, as Pygmalion did with his statue. I can forgive Pygmalion, for what he produced was a masterpiece.

At the beginning of September, Montcalm, accompanied by Bougainville, left Montreal for Fort Carillon (Ticonderoga), to speed up work on the defences and to send out reconnaissance parties in the direction of the British Fort William Henry, against which an expedition was planned for the following season. The British had massed 10,000 men between Fort Edward and Fort William Henry, with their base at Albany at the head of Lake George. Montcalm faced them at Carillon with 5,300 regulars and Canadians, in a position where they could defy three times their number; but Montcalm thought no more of stirring than did Loudon, the British Commander-in-Chief. Each stood watching the other, with the lake between them until the season closed. Indian war parties, however, urged on by the French, continued to ravage the western borders with the tomahawk.

Vaudreuil wrote despatch after despatch to the Minister at Versailles, taking credit for the number of war-parties that his officers kept at work, and filling page upon page with details of the coups they had struck: how one had brought in two English scalps; another, one; another, seven. He owns that they committed frightful atrocities, mutilating and even burning their prisoners, including women and children; but he expresses no regret and probably felt none, since he declares that the object of this murderous warfare was to punish the English until they longed for peace. The British too, but with less success, having fewer Indians, led war-parties, from which they required not scalps but prisoners, as sources of information. However, the pro-British Indians were often beyond control and inflicted atrocities every bit as horrible as those the pro-French Indians perpetrated, even resorting to cannibalism.

On 19 September the British Captain Hodges, with fifty men, was ambushed a few miles from Fort William Henry by some 160 Canadians and Indians. Among the leaders of the Canadians—a wild crew, bedecked and bedaubed like their Indian companions—was the famous bushranger Marin, and Bougainville. Already alerted of Hodge's presence in the area, the party had set out in canoes on the evening of the 16th, had passed in the gloom under the steeps of Roger's Rock, and had landed on the western shore. From there scouts were sent out to reconnoitre. On their return the following day, one of their number called all the chiefs to council. Bougainville, observing his strange companions with an interest not unmixed with disgust, describes them as they stalked gravely to the meeting place, wrapped in coloured blankets with spears in their hands. "Of all caprice," he writes, "Indian caprice is the most capricious." They were, he says, insolent to the French, made rules for them which they themselves did not keep, and compelled the whole party to move when and where they pleased. That night, the Indian scouts reported that they had seen fires of an encampment on the western shore. An hour before dawn the whole party advanced to the attack, filing silently under the dark arches of the forest, the Indians all but naked and streaked with their war-paint of vermilion and soot. When they reached the spot, they found only the smouldering fires of a deserted bivouac. Then followed a consultation, ending, after much dispute, with the choice by the Indians of 110 of their most active warriors to attempt some stroke in the neighbourhood of the British fort. Marin joined them with thirty Canadians, while the rest, including Bougainville, encamped to await the result. At night the war party returned, raising the death cry and firing their guns, boasting that they had surprised and killed fifty-three Englishmen.

"The very recital of the cruelties they committed", wrote Bougainville, "is horrible; the ferocity and insolence of these black-souled barbarians makes one shudder. It is an abominable kind of war; reprisals as a system are terrible and in such an atmosphere callousness is infectious."

This was only one of the many war-parties sent out that year from Ticonderoga to which Bougainville was assigned. Vaudreuil, not so sensitive as the young French captain, believed in Indians and continued to send them to

Ticonderoga in numbers that were sometimes embarrassing. Even the Pot-
tawattamies from as far off as Lake Michigan were prowling around Fort
William Henry silently killing the sentries with their arrows, while their
medicine men remained at Ticonderoga practising sorcery and divination.
Bougainville wrote in his Journal on 15 October,

> Yesterday the old Pottawattamies who have stayed here "made
> medicine" to get news of their brethren. The lodge trembled, the
> sorcerer sweated drops of blood and the devil came at last and told
> him that the warriors would come back with scalps and prisoners. A
> sorcerer in the medicine lodge is exactly like the Pythoness on the
> tripod or the witch Canidia invoking the shades.

All this time, while Bougainville was engaged on these dangerous reconnaissances, work on Fort Carillon was proceeding, under the direction of the
Canadian engineer Lotbinière. However, despite Montcalm's initial injection
of energy, progress was at snail's pace, leading Bougainville to complain,

> The business goes on but slowly. The soldiery, corrupted by the
> amount of money they receive here, and the example set by the
> savages and Canadians, and breathing an atmosphere redolent of
> independence, work without enthusiasm. The engineer is scarcely
> ever on the job. It is in his interest to see that the fort is not completed
> punctually. He has the exclusive privilege of selling wine (he sells it at
> fifty-five *sols* a bottle), and all the workmen's money, even the pay of
> his troops, flows into his canteen. . . . The soldiers have too much
> money. Yesterday a soldier from Languedoc [the regiment of that
> name] lost 100 louis at play. This country is dangerous to discipline. . . .

Further on he writes,

> I am amazed by the steadfastness and industry with which everyone
> here seizes every possible opportunity of making free with the King's
> money. . . . When I reflect on the methods of governing this country,
> for which the King pays out enormous sums, I recall the way Jupiter
> ruled the world as described at Lucian's feast.

At the end of October, as winter started to set its icy grip over New England
and the Great Lakes, the French began to withdraw towards Canada, leaving
Ticonderoga in the keeping of five or six companies. The British provincial
garrison of Fort William Henry too marched home, their ranks thinned by
scurvy and smallpox, to be replaced by some 400 regulars from Britain.

On 26 October, Montcalm, accompanied by Bougainville, returned to winter-quarters on the banks of the St Lawrence. The weather was misty and an infinite sadness brooded over the countryside. Bougainville was exhausted by the fatigues of the campaign, by his many reconnaissances and by the atrocities he had witnessed. On his arrival at Montreal, therefore, Montcalm gave him leave of absence to visit his cousin M. de Lienne in Quebec, the same who had shown him hospitality on his arrival in New France. From there he wrote a long letter to his brother:

> I am tired out with this campaign. Since my arrival in Canada I have travelled close upon 500 leagues [approximately 1500 miles]. The continual travelling, the poor food, the frequent lack of sleep, the nights spent under the open sky in the woods, the expeditions with the Indians, have affected my chest a little. At the end of last month I even spat blood. Diet and rest will set me up and make me fit to start off again in the spring. As far as that goes, I was by no means the only one to suffer from the hardships of the campaign. M. de Montcalm's health has also been greatly affected by it. One needs an iron constitution not to feel the effects of such endurance. I continue to be on excellent terms with my general, who overwhelms me with kindness. I have done all in my power to satisfy him; and he ought to be content with the results of his campaign, for it has been both fortunate and brilliant, since although inferior in numbers, we have captured from the English one of the most important positions in the country, while they have not been able to break through our defences in one single case. Let us hope that this campaign and the successes we have achieved in Europe will win peace for us! Here we desire it more than anyone. What a country and what people, my dear brother, and what patience is needed to put up with the aversion they are pleased to feel for us. . . . All I can say is that when the time comes to leave this country, we shall sing with all our hearts, In exitu Israel.

The winter, in spite of its exceptional severity, allowed Bougainville to lead a more normal life and enjoy the benefits of civilization. He found Quebec as fine as any town of its size in France. He moved in society, thoroughly enjoyed female company and playing at faro for high stakes. Montcalm, who kept a fatherly eye on him, wrote that, while he disapproved of extravagance and wasteful expenditure of public funds, he had no objection to Bougainville gambling with his private money if he could afford it. He even kept a note of Bougainville's gains and losses. Bougainville broke more or less even, slightly to his advantage. Vaudreuil, who was extremely critical of the gambling among French officers, seemed oblivious of the fact that most of the gambling was carried on at

B

receptions given by his own intendant, Bigot, who as we know was amassing a fortune by fraudulent exploitation of government funds.

But Bougainville by no means spent all his time playing faro and attending routs. "I spend my time reading, writing and meditating. Without Montaigne, without Horace, Virgil, Tacitus, Montesquieu and Corneille, without the companionship and sympathy of my general, weariness would have overcome me utterly", he wrote to Mme Hérault. This was no exaggeration. He was also busy adding to his treatise on integral calculus—"a very demanding task", as he says—and working on his notes on Indian customs and their language, and on the character of the *habitants* (the Canadian word for settlers) and the country. He even made notes on the rock formations of the St Lawrence gorges. In a letter to the Minister of War Montcalm wrote,

> I never lose an opportunity of informing myself about this little-known country. M. de Bougainville, with whose powers of discernment you are already familiar, works even harder than I to complete this subject, and perhaps one day we may prove of use to this colony by submitting to an enlightened minister a report which would never have seen the light of day had he [Bougainville] not come here. He communicates his ideas to me and we discuss them together. . . .

Bougainville was in fact to send his *Mémoires sur l'état de la Nouvelle France* first to Mme Hérault for transmission to the Minister for War. The report clearly reflects both his own and Montcalm's views: "What a colony! What a people! What benefits a Colbert could draw from it!"

The picture which Bougainville drew of La Nouvelle France certainly owed its inspiration to Colbert and Vauban.

> Canada must be populated. To achieve this all soldiers must be permitted to marry and each given four arpents [1 arpent=approx. 125 acres], a cow, a ewe, an axe, a mattock and two years' pay. All vagabonds from large towns should be sent here on board ships leaving France, at the rate of four persons per 100 tons. Fertile lands, healthy air, charming climate, abundant game, what more is needed to establish oneself between Lake Erie and Lake Huron, as far as Detroit, which although it at present has only 200 inhabitants, could become a large town, since it serves as an entrepôt for the many Indian tribes, who flock there each year . . . with their merchandise. . . .

Bougainville then goes on to describe the network of forts, or trading posts, and the Indian tribes with which these often distant outposts traded, and of the twice-yearly transport of grain by barge down the Mississippi to Louisiana. He also mentions a strange "tribe" of bearded white men living on the banks of the

Missouri "who have villages fortified in the European style, with palisaded bastions surrounded by moats". These Mandans, as they were called, may well have been descendants of Scandinavian colonists established in Greenland in the Middle Ages, or even those Northmen established in Vinland by Eric the Red in AD 968. Of the French Canadian colonists he writes,

> The simple *habitants* would be scandalized to hear themselves referred to as "peasants". Indeed they are made of better stuff; they have more intelligence, more education than those of France. This is because they pay no taxes, because they are free to hunt and fish and because they live in a state of independence. They are brave. Their type of courage, similar to that of the Indians, is to expose themselves as little as possible and to lie in ambush. They are good when fighting in the woods and are excellent marksmen; when fighting they disperse and take cover behind trees. That is how they defeated General Braddock. . . . It must be admitted that the savages are their superiors in this type of warfare, and it is the affection that they [the Indians] show us which up to now has saved Canada. The Canadian is haughty, vainglorious, a liar, obliging, affable, honest, an indefatigable hunter, runner and traveller, but a lazy husbandman. Among Canadians, those from Quebec are the best navigators, those that travel in the Pays d'en Haut are the bravest. There are hardly any poor in Canada: hospitals are only for the sick; almshouses only encourage idleness. . . .

Towards the end of January, Bougainville had already resumed active service with Montcalm, who was preparing for the summer campaign against Fort William Henry. However, in February, Vaudreuil, anxious to forestall Montcalm and crown himself with laurels without the aid of French regulars, sent a detachment (Vaudreuil called it an army), composed almost entirely of Canadian rangers and Indians, under the command of his brother Rigaud, to capture the fort. No pains were spared to equip the force: it was said that no less than 1 million francs had been made available for the purpose. To give Vaudreuil his due, the expedition had a good chance of success. The garrison of Fort William Henry had been reduced by sickness to 270 men—a mere winter "caretaker" garrison—while Rigaud had at his disposal 1,600 Canadians and Indians, including reinforcements from Ticonderoga. Nor was Vaudreuil altogether at fault in selecting Canadians and Indians to the exclusion of regular French troops, unaccustomed as the latter were to the severity of Canadian winters and unfamiliar with the use of snowshoes. Where he was at fault was in not having taken Montcalm into his confidence; in fact, it was only after all plans for the expedition had been drawn up that he sent his secretary to the General "with the instructions he had given to his brother, which he had hitherto withheld" (wrote Montcalm). Moreover, he had overlooked the fact that, while Canadian

rangers and Indians were excellent in forest warfare, they were not suited for a
resolute attack on a fortified position. Surprise, and surprise alone in this case,
could have insured success.

After reaching Ticonderoga, where Rigaud picked up his reinforcements
and scaling ladders, he marched his force for three days over icebound, snow-
covered Lake George and arrived off Fort William Henry on the evening of 18
March. Certainly the British garrison had never expected a large-scale attack in
the depths of winter, but the element of surprise was lost. The approach of the
Canadians had been heard and the British cannon were trained on the ice. Twice
the Canadians were driven back. On the following night, however, a small
detachment of Rigaud's men approached close enough to burn two icebound
British sloops and a number of *bateaux*. On Sunday the 20th, since all element of
surprise had been lost, Rigaud, hoping to intimidate the garrison into surrender
by an ostentatious show of strength, despatched a force across the ice carrying
their scaling-ladders and showing themselves to the best effect. They stopped at
a safe distance, facing the fort, while several of them advanced waving a red flag
—red because the Bourbon flag was white. A British officer with a few men went
out to meet them and returned to the fort with Le Mercier,[3] commanding the
Canadian artillery, who announced himself as bearer of a message from Rigaud.
Le Mercier was taken before Major Eyre, commander of the fort. After the
usual exchange of courtesies, he invited Eyre to give up the place peaceably,
promising the most favourable terms and threatening a general assault and
massacre in case of refusal. Eyre replied that he would defend himself to the last
and the envoy was escorted back.

The British now steeled themselves for the expected assault, but when the
attack came it was not against the fort but against outbuildings—storehouses, a
hospital, and a sawmill. Before morning nearly all the buildings were ablaze. No
further action took place until Tuesday morning, when a few volunteers made
a bold attempt to fire a sloop still on the stocks, and to destroy those buildings that
had so far escaped destruction. In this they were only partly successful; but they
set fire to the sloop and some neighbouring huts. They then stood far out on the
ice watching the blazing vessel, a superb bonfire amid the wilderness of snow.

On Wednesday morning, as the sun rose bright on a scene of wintry
splendour, the British saw with surprise the lake dotted with Rigaud's retreating
followers, toiling towards Canada on snowshoes. Before they reached their
base, many of them were temporarily blinded by the insufferable glare and were
led homeward holding hands with their comrades.

So much for Vaudreuil's victory, as he called it.

Writing of the expedition, Bougainville ironically commented in his
Journal,

> On 20 March, in full view of the English, Rigaud's force crossed Lake
> George in procession, every member of the detachment ostentatiously

carrying a ladder, while M. le Mercier went off to summon the commandant of the fort to surrender. M. le Mercier reminded the commandant that it was the usage among civilized nations, in order to avoid unnecessary slaughter, to give warning before beginning an escalade, and that he would be well advised to surrender the fortress and not persist in the defence of territory rightly belonging to the King of France. The besieged must have laughed at such an ultimatum, for the besieger had ignored the fact that the success of an escalade depends upon its surprise and that, when war is once declared, rights of ownership or pretensions thereto no longer count for anything. In a word, it is not enough to be an astute man in peace to avoid making a fool of oneself in war. The English officer, after calling together the officers of his garrison (merely to gain time to remove the ammunition from outlying magazines), replied that he would defend himself to the last. . . . The English in short had taken advantage of our negligence to empty the ammunition sheds, so that any outbreak of fire would not spread to the fort.

Bougainville had no great opinion of Canadian tactics and initiative and one cannot help but feel (since the losses on both sides were minimal) that he was not altogether displeased with Rigaud's failure.

Chapter Three

The Second Campaign, 1759

Following one of the severest winters so far recorded in Canada, the spring of 1757 ushered in further hardship. Famine threatened the land. The influx into Montreal, before the New Year, of Indian tribes offering to raise the hatchet on behalf of France, and in return expecting to be fed and supplied with copious quantities of brandy and victuals, had contributed greatly to the general shortage. The lack of organization and the corruption in the Commissary's department added to the general distress. Belatedly Vaudreuil ordered curés and militia captains to scour the country in search of provisions for the forthcoming summer campaign. Enough corn and bacon to feed 12,000 soldiers for a month was found stored by the *habitants*. Vaudreuil, while disliking the French regulars, felt that he could not dispense with them, and before the winter months had set in he had called upon France to provide further men, food and munitions. His request was granted, and 2,400 men were ordered to Canada to strengthen the colonial and French forces there. However it was learnt that the British too were sending reinforcements. But, whereas Vaudreuil's objective was to strike the British at their frontier posts of Fort William Henry and Fort Edward (at the head of Lake George), Lord Loudon, the British Commander-in-Chief, had the previous autumn proposed a scheme that, while involving a possible attack on Quebec, had as its immediate object the reduction of Louisbourg—an important objective no doubt, but one that had no bearing on the main question: that of who controlled the interior of the continent. For this purpose he had withdrawn the best part of his troops from the northern frontier to New York, where they awaited the arrival of the British fleet to transport them to Louisbourg.

This is not the place to enter into detail about the disastrous Louisbourg expedition, since it had no direct bearing on Bougainville's career. All that need be said here is that Loudon's ill-starred attempt and the drawing off of the British forces from the frontier, where they were needed most, did for France more than she could have done for herself and gave Montcalm and Vaudreuil the opportunity to execute the scheme they had been nursing since the fall of Oswego. Bougainville wrote to Mme Hérault,

All I can tell you is that two sieges, as well as a battle, figure on the programme we expect to carry through, and that your child shudders at the thought of the horrors he will be forced to witness. Only with the greatest difficulty are we able to keep in check these savages from the furthermost backwoods; they are the most notorious cannibals among all the tribes and surely the most ferocious of all mankind. Listen to what their chiefs had to say to Monsieur de Montcalm three days ago. "It is no good counting on us, my father, to give quarter to the English. We have among us young braves who have not yet tasted of their "broth" (i.e. blood). Fresh meat has brought them from the ends of the world. They must learn to handle the knife and plunge it into English hearts!" So much for our comrades, *ma chère maman*. What a rabble, what a sight for sensitive souls.

In another letter to his brother he wrote,

We have close upon 8,000 men, among them 1,800 naked savages, some black, some red, all yelling, shrieking, dancing, chanting war songs, getting drunk and crying out for "broth", that is to say blood, who have been lured five hundred leagues by the smell of fresh meat and the opportunity of teaching their youth how to carve up a human body fit for the cauldron. Such are the companions who shadow our every movement night and day. I shudder to think of the terrible scenes that I shall be forced to witness.

The events that followed fully bore out Bougainville's worst fears. Rousseau's myth of the "noble savage" was to be exploded.

More and more Indians from north and west, enticed by the prospect of gifts, scalps and plunder, continued to pour into Montreal eager to fight for France. All were anxious to see Montcalm, whose victory over the British at Oswego had inflamed their imaginations. One day, in the course of a ceremonial visit, Bougainville records, an Indian chief addressed the General as follows: "We wanted to see this famous man who tramples the English under his feet. We thought to find him so tall that his head would be lost in the clouds. But you are a little man, my father. It is when we look into your eyes that we see the greatness of the pine tree and the fire of the eagle."

Although the pagan Indians had flocked to fight under the French banner, it still remained to secure the co-operation of the Mission Indians, both in and around the colony. To this end Montcalm, accompanied by Bougainville, Rigaud and others, set out to sing the war-song with the converts of the Two Mountains. The General was greeted by a salute of musketry and then conducted to a grand council lodge, where the circle of wild and savage faces, half seen in the dim light of a few candles and the flickering flames of a fire, over

which was suspended a cauldron, suggested to Bougainville an assembly of
sorcerers. He wrote, "I sang the war-song in the name of M. de Montcalm and
was much applauded. It consisted of nothing but the words, 'Let us trample the
English under our feet', chanted over and over again. Then followed a great
feast, at which two oxen, supplied by the General, were devoured."

The next day, the ceremony was repeated by the Indians of Saut St Louis.
There too, Bougainville sang the war-song; once again there was a great feast,
and with one voice the warriors swore to fight on behalf of France. Bougainville's performance was acclaimed with such enthusiasm that he was adopted
by the tribe of the Turtle. He wrote to Madame Hérault,

> I have greatly added to the number of your family, and without
> undue boastfulness, I think I can claim to have provided you with
> some pretty abominable relatives. The Iroquois of Saut St Louis have
> made your adopted child one of themselves and have named him
> Garioniatsigoa, which means "Wrath of the Great Heavens". Has my
> angelic countenance actually so baleful an expression? . . . You behold
> me then a war chief of the Iroquois. . . . I was displayed to the entire
> nation, offered the first morsel at the feast and sang my war-song in
> duet with the Chief of Chiefs, while the rest dedicated their own
> songs to me. I have made the rounds of all my family and distributed
> the wherewithal for a feast to be held in every cabin.

Bougainville also described a service, held in the Mission Church of Le Saut, at
which squaws and warriors sang in the choir. He was much impressed by the
quality of their singing, finding them "more melodious than our nuns at home".
He at least had the consolation that his new family were not cannibals and were
comparatively civilized, and that their main preoccupation was the breaking-in
of horses. He describes the village as "the Newmarket of Canada". It was neat
and tidy and the natives grew crops and vegetables, raised fowls, and traded
"just like Frenchmen".

Meanwhile troops, Canadians and Indians, were moving by detachments
up Lake Champlain. Fleets of *bateaux* and canoes followed each other day by
day along the capricious lake, in calm or storm, sunshine or rain, till, towards
the end of July, the whole force was gathered at Ticonderoga. Francis Parkman
writes,

> Here was gathered a martial population of eight thousand men
> including the brightest civilization and the darkest barbarism: from
> the scholar-soldier Montcalm and his no less accomplished aide de
> camp, Bougainville; from de Lévis, conspicuous for graces of person;
> from a throng of courtly young officers, who would have seemed out
> of place in that wilderness had they not done their work so well in it;

from these to the foulest man-eating savage of the uttermost north-west. (*Montcalm and Wolfe*, vol I.)

Of Indian allies Bougainville recorded,

> There were nearly 2,000. One of the tribes—the Iowas—spoke a language which no one understood; they all bivouacked where they saw fit, for discipline was a word unknown to them. Only the Mission Indians accepted some sort of authority, from their priests who accompanied them. For the rest, their religion is brute paganism. I will say it once for all, one must be the slave of these savages, listen to them day and night, in council and in private, whenever the fancy takes them, or whenever a dream, a fit of the vapours, or their perpetual craving for brandy gets possession of them. Besides which, they are always wanting something for their equipment, arms or toilet, and the general of the army must give orders for the smallest trifle—an eternal, wearisome detail, of which one can have no idea in Europe.

Nor was it easy to keep such a mob fed. Rations sufficient for a week would be served to them, but in three days they would have consumed them and be back for more. On one occasion, Bougainville tells us, they took the matter into their own hands and butchered and devoured eighteen head of cattle intended for the regular troops, "nor did any officer dare oppose this St Bartholomew's Day of oxen". "Their paradise is to be drunk", he goes on to say. "Their paradise, however, can be Hell, for sometimes, mad with brandy, they grapple and tear each other with their teeth like wolves." On one occasion, he tells us in his Journal, citing the *Lettre de Père Roubaud*, a French missionary attached to the army saw a large number of Ottawa Indians squatting about a fire, before which meat was roasting on sticks stuck in the ground. On approaching, he saw that it was the flesh of an Englishman, other parts of whom were boiling in a kettle, while nearby sat eight or ten English prisoners, forced to watch their comrade devoured. The horror-stricken priest began to remonstrate, but was interrupted by a young brave who replied angrily in broken French, "You have French taste; I have Indian. This is good meat for me", and pressed him to share it.

Bougainville continues,

> This abomination could not be prevented: . . . if force had been used to stop it, all the Ottawa Indians would have gone home in a rage. They were therefore left to finish their meal undisturbed. Having eaten one of their prisoners, they began to treat the rest with the utmost kindness, bringing them white bread and attending to all their wants—a seeming change of heart owing to the fact that they were a valuable

commodity for which their owners hoped to get a good price at
Montreal. M. de Montcalm wished to send them thither at once, to
which, after a long debate, the Indians consented, demanding however, a receipt in full and bargaining that the captives be supplied with
shoes and blankets.

These prisoners were part of a detachment sent from Fort William Henry to
reconnoitre the French outposts. As they had paddled down the lake, close
inshore, they had been met by a deadly volley of musketry from the bush-clad
banks, while a swarm of canoes darted out on them. These New Jersey men
were seized with such a panic that some jumped into the water to escape, while
the Indians leapt after them and speared them like fish; other Indians swam
under water and ripped open the birch-bark canoes with their scalping knives.
"Terrified", says Bougainville, "by the sight of these monsters, their agility,
their firing and their yells, the New Jersey men surrendered almost without
resistance." About a hundred, however, made their escape. The rest were
killed or captured and three of the bodies were eaten on the spot. So elated were
the Indians by this victory that they became insupportable; "but", adds Bougainville, "here in the forests of America we can no more do without them than
without cavalry on the plain".

Meanwhile preparations for the attack on Fort William Henry were being
urged on with the greatest energy. On the eve of departure Montcalm, anxious
for harmony among his redskin allies, had called them together to a grand
council. Forty-one tribes and sub-tribes, Christian and heathen, from the east
and from the west, were represented—979 chiefs and warriors, men of the
forests and men of the plains, hunters of moose and hunters of buffalo, some
bearing steel hatchets, some with stone war-clubs, some armed with French
guns, others with bows and flint-headed arrows. Bougainville describes how
all sat down in silence, decked out with ceremonial war-paint, scalp locks, eagle
plumes or buffalo horns, the French officers, dressed in white uniforms, crowding round to observe this extraordinary spectacle. Then Montcalm addressed
the gathering and the various interpreters passed on his words.

"Children, I am delighted to see you all joined in this good work. So
long as you remain one, the English cannot resist you. The great King has
sent me to protect and defend you; but above all he has charged me to make
you happy and unconquerable, by establishing among you the union
which ought to prevail among brothers, children of one father, the great
Onontio."

Then he held out a huge wampum belt of six thousand beads.

"Take this sacred pledge of his word. The union of the beads of which it is
made is the sign of your united strength. By it I bind you all together, so that
none of you can separate from the rest until the English are defeated and their
fort destroyed."

Montcalm's speech (quoted here from Bougainville's Journal) was universally acclaimed and the council closed in perfect harmony.

Montcalm then sent a circular to his regular officers, urging them to dispense
for a while with all luxuries, even comforts. Everything not absolutely necessary
should be left behind; a canvas shelter to every two officers should serve
them as a tent, and a bearskin as a bed. "Yet I don't forbid a mattress",
he added. "Age and infirmity may make it necessary for some; but I shall
not have one myself and have no doubt that all who can will willingly imitate
me."

Since there were insufficient *bateaux* to carry the whole force, the Chevalier
de Lévis was ordered to march by the lakeside with 2,500 men, Canadians,
French regulars and Indians. He set out on 30 July, his men carrying nothing
but knapsacks, blankets and weapons. The heat was intolerable, the way
extremely tough; two officers broke down completely. On 1 August, Montcalm, accompanied by Bougainville, embarked with all his remaining force.
First came canoes filled with painted savages; next 250 *bateaux*, moved by sail
and oar, bearing the Canadian militia and battalions of French and colonial
regulars; then cannon and mortars, each on a platform sustained by two *bateaux*
lashed together; after that, more French regulars, followed by provision-
bateaux and the field hospital; and, lastly, a rearguard of regulars.

On 3 August the whole force had disembarked and was bivouacked to the
right of the fort, hidden from view by what is still called Artillery Point. On
the following morning the French camp was astir. The column of de Lévis, led
by Indians, moved towards the fort, while Montcalm followed with the main
body. Next, the artillery rounded the point, while a host of Indians put out
onto the lake, ranged their canoes abreast from shore to shore, and then advanced slowly, with rhythmic paddle-strokes, shouting defiance.

The enemy's position was in full view before them. At the head of the lake,
towards the right, stood the fort, close to the edge of the water. On its left was
a marsh, then some rough ground, beyond which was a low, rocky hill,
crowned with an entrenched camp. All round the fort the forest had been cut
down and burned, to give a clear field of fire. The fort itself was an irregular
bastioned square, formed by embankments of gravel surmounted by a rampart
of heavy logs laid in tiers, crossed one upon another, the interstices filled with
earth. It was protected by the lake to the north, the marsh on the east, and to
the south and west by ditches with *chevaux-de-frise* (iron spikes set in timber to
repel horses). The fort's armament consisted of seventeen cannon as well as
mortars and swivel guns; six more guns defended the entrenched camp. Fourteen miles distant lay Fort Edward, where General Webb was encamped with
2,600 men, mostly provincials.

The action began with some skirmishing when the British tried to drive
their cattle to safety and destroy some outbuildings that might have provided
cover for their attackers. In the meantime, a force of Indians was ordered to

cover the road leading to Fort Edward, while de Lévis encamped hard by, to
support them. The skirmishing over, Montcalm proceeded to examine the
ground and decide on his plan of attack. He made his way to the rear of the
entrenched camp, which he hoped to carry by assault, but it had a breastwork
of stones and logs and he thought the attempt too hazardous. Instead he decided
to lay siege to the main fort in the conventional manner.

All the while Indian scouting parties were on the watch to report on any
move that General Webb might make to come to the relief of Lieutenant-
Colonel Munro (or Monroe), the tough old Scot commanding Fort William
Henry. Apropos of these scouting parties, Bougainville, always the classical
scholar, noted in his journal,

> Prior to making a reconnaissance, the Indian chiefs of those detailed
> for the task came to bring M. de Montcalm as many sticks of wood as
> there were braves assigned for these missions, a ceremony they always
> observe when they wish to strike a blow. It is a muster role of the
> party. Thus in the early days of the Persian monarchy, when they
> went to war, each warrior placed an arrow in some public place.
> Upon their return, each took up his arrow again, and what remained
> showed what loss they had suffered.

Having made his preparations, Montcalm sent one of his aides-de-camp with a
letter to Munro. "I owe it to humanity to summon you to surrender. At
present I can restrain the savages, and make them observe the terms of capitulation, as I might not under other circumstances; an obstinate deference on your
part could only retard the capture of the place by a few days . . . in view of the
dispositions I have made. I demand a decisive answer within an hour." Munro's
reply was that he and his soldiers would defend themselves to the last.

On the night of 4 August, the French opened their first entrenchments—a
task of the greatest difficulty, as the ground was covered with a profusion of
half-burned tree-stumps, roots, branches and fallen trees. 800 men toiled day
and night under a hail of grapeshot from the British guns. Remarkably, there
were few casualties, for the French had worked so hard and quickly, that they
were soon under cover. On the seventh, Indian scouts shot down a runner
coming from Fort Edward. In the runner's clothing was found a letter from
General Webb to Munro, in which he promised assistance should the militia he
had requested from New York arrive in time. In the meantime he exhorted
Munro to defend the fort with all the vigour at his command, but hinted that,
if capitulation should become inevitable, he would do well to secure the most
honourable terms he could in good time, rather than wait until sheer necessity
forced him to surrender.

On the following day Montcalm sent Bougainville to deliver General
Webb's intercepted message to Munro, to which he added a personal note once

again advising the commandant not to prolong the defence until the last moment. Bougainville relates how he carried out his mission:

> Preceded by a standard-bearer carrying a red flag and a drummer beating a tattoo, and accompanied by an escort of eighteen grenadiers, I emerged from the trench. At the foot of the glacis the English summoned me to halt, while an officer and fifteen grenadiers approached to inquire my business. Upon my answering that I was the bearer of a letter from my general to the British Commandant, two more officers emerged from the fort, one of whom remained on guard over my grenadiers, while the other, after bandaging my eyes, conducted me to the entrenched camp, where I presented the letters of both the Marquis de Montcalm and General Webb to the commandant. Profuse thanks and appreciation of French courtesy, protestations of delight at having to treat with so generous a foe—such were the contents of General [sic] Munro's reply to the Marquis de Montcalm. Again, with my eyes bandaged, I was led beyond the precincts of the fort, and then, as soon as our fellows judged that the grenadiers had had time enough to retire into the fort, the fire from our batteries started up again.

Though Munro had decided still to hold out, his position was untenable. More than 300 of his men had been killed and wounded, smallpox was raging in the fort, and the casemates were crowded with sick. A sortie from the entrenched camp and another from the fort had been repulsed with loss. All the British heavy guns had been put out of action by the French artillery; the forts ramparts were rapidly being demolished, and it was clear that a breach would soon be made for an assault. At seven in the morning of 9 August a white flag was hoisted in token of surrender.

Bougainville writes in his Journal,

> Colonel Young came to propose articles of capitulation to de Montcalm. I was sent to draw them up and take the first steps to put them into operation.

In substance the capitulation provided that the troops, both of the fort and entrenched camp, to the number of 2,000 men, should depart with honours of war with the baggage of officers and soldiers alike; and that they should be conducted to Fort Lydius[4] escorted by a detachment of French troops and by the principal officers and interpreters attached to the Indians; that until the return of this escort an officer should remain in French hands as hostage; that the troops would not serve for eighteen months against His Most Christian Majesty, nor against his allies; that within three months all French,

Canadian and Indian prisoners taken on land in North America since the commencement of the war should be returned to French forts; that the artillery, vessels and all the munitions and provisions would belong to His Most Christian Majesty, except one six-pounder, which the Marquis de Montcalm granted Colonel Munro and the garrison as witness of his esteem for the fine defence they had made.

Before signing the capitulation, Montcalm assembled a council of Indian chiefs. After informing them of the articles granted to the besieged, and of the motives that had determined his according them, he asked their consent and their promise that their young men would not commit any disorder. The chiefs agreed to everything and promised to restrain their braves.

"One sees by this action of the M. de Montcalm to what point one is a slave to Indians in this country. They are a necessary evil", wrote Bougainville.

The garrison then evacuated the fort and marched to join their comrades in the entrenched camp, which was included in the surrender. No sooner were they gone than the Indians clambered through the embrasures in search of rum and plunder. All the sick unable to leave their beds were butchered. The Indians, drunk with blood-lust, next turned their attention to the entrenched camp. The French guards stationed there were powerless to keep out the rabble.

> They roamed among the tents, intrusive and insolent, their faces be-daubed with war-paint, grinning like fiends as they handled in anticipation of the knife the long hair of women, of whom, as well as of children, there were many in the camp, all crazed with fright. The Indians wanted to plunder the chests of the English; the latter resisted; and there was fear that serious disorder would ensue. The Marquis de Montcalm ran thither immediately and used every means to restore tranquillity. . . . The Marquis spared no efforts to prevent the rapacity of the savages and, I am forced to say of certain persons associated with them. [Bougainville is referring to the Canadian interpreters and officers attached to the tribes.] At last, at nine o'clock, order seemed to be restored. The Marquis even induced the Indians to promise that, besides the escort agreed upon in the capitulation terms, two chiefs of each tribe should accompany the English on their way to Fort Edward.

Bougainville was not to see what followed, for Montcalm now sent him to Montreal to carry news of the victory. What did ensue was appalling. For details of the massacre that followed, I refer readers to Francis Parkman's *Montcalm and Wolfe*, vol. I, pp. 509–15. In brief, after a night of fear and appre-hension, the terrified British, impatient to reach the safety of Fort Edward, started out at dawn, without even awaiting their escort. This was the signal for the Indians to run amok. Men, women and children were scalped, tomahawked, stripped and dragged off into the forest, while many of the Canadian militia stood by apparently indifferent. Montcalm, de Lévis and de Bourlamaque and many other French officers, who had hastened from their camp at the first news of disaster, threw themselves among the Indians, often at the risk of their own lives, in an attempt to allay their frenzy. Montcalm, throwing off his coat and baring his chest, shouted, "Kill me, but spare the English who are under my protection", but to no avail.

How many British were killed it is impossible to say with any exactness, but it is at least certain that 600–700 were carried off, stripped or otherwise mal-treated. Montcalm succeeded in recovering more than 400 in the course of the day. Many of the French officers did what they could to relieve the wants of the British by buying back from their captors the clothing that had been torn from them. Many of the fugitives had taken refuge in the fort. There Father Roubaud, a Jesuit missionary in charge of the "Christian" Abenakis, who were held to be responsible for starting the massacre, records that he found a crowd of half-frenzied women crying in anguish for husbands and children. All the refugees and ransomed prisoners were afterwards conducted to the entrenched camp, where they were provided with food and shelter and an adequate guard of French regulars for their protection. On the 15th they were sent to Fort Edward, under a strong escort.

On the morning following the massacre, the Indians decamped in a body and set out for Montreal carrying with them their plunder and some 200 prisoners, whom they refused to release, believing that they would receive a higher ransom for them in the capital. On 15 August, the French soldiers were set to work demolishing the fort and barracks; the huge logs of the rampart were thrown into a mighty heap. The dead bodies recovered from the casemates were added to the pile and the whole was set on fire. The gigantic funeral pyre blazed all night. Then, on the 16th, the army re-embarked. "The din of ten thousand combatants, the rage, the terror, the agony, were gone: and no living thing was left but the wolves that gathered from the mountains to feast upon the dead" (Parkman, *Montcalm and Wolfe*, vol. I, p. 513).

Chapter Four

Winter-Quarters

An exhausted Bougainville made all haste to carry the news of his general's victory to Montreal. How fortunate for this sensitive young officer that he had not been a witness to the horrors of the massacre, for he was utterly worn out and admits that he had twice collapsed in a dead faint during the siege. To Mme Hérault he wrote,

> I am back from the wars, *ma chère maman*, the bearer of glad tidings and charged by my general, who has not the time, to write to the two ministers giving them all details. . . . I am leaving again for Carillon almost immediately, but I am, truth to tell, very tired. I spent twenty nights without undressing, badly fed, with the ground for a bed. . . . The change of ministry [Mme Hérault's brother-in-law, de Moras, had recently been appointed to the Marine] has not improved my relations with Monsieur de Vaudreuil. I do not know what I have done to turn him against me. . . . Is it because I see too clearly, because I am not dazzled by appearances, because I am beginning to learn a little? Because he disapproves of my attachment to a person to whom I am in duty bound? In all this, *chère maman*, can you find cause to grumble at your son? I cannot reproach myself with any indiscretion or impertinence.
>
> I feel obliged, as far as possible, to keep myself informed of everything that goes on in this colony. You may be sure that everything I say shall be the truth. . . .

Bougainville then goes on to tell of the lamentable aftermath of the capture of Fort William Henry.

> Would you believe that this abominable action of the Indians at Fort William had accomplices among people who call themselves Frenchmen; that greed for gain, the certainty of getting very cheaply from Indians all the goods they had pillaged, are the primary causes of a horror for which England will not fail to reproach us for a long time

The author's painting of the Basse Ville of Quebec as it appeared to Bougainville, from a contemporary engraving.

Michael Ross

to come? Thank Heaven, our own officers are blameless in this respect; several risked their lives on this occasion; they divided up everything they had with the unfortunate survivors. The English say that if ever they have occasion to besiege and capture us, there will be two capitulations—one for the French troops, the other for the Canadians. These are frightful truths, *chère maman*. But sights still more frightful have befouled my eyes and left an ineffaceable bitterness in my soul. May the memories of these abominations vanish. What a land! What a people! . . . Will my exile last long? In the name of the friendship you have always been kind enough to show me, do your best, *chère maman*, to see that, should the war last, my next campaign will be my last in this country. Whether I am promoted or not is all the same to me, so long as I see you and France again. ; . . Adieu. Your poor Iroquois loves you with all his heart.

About the same time, Bougainville also wrote to his brother:

The English openly praise the actions of the French regulars, but these savages and these others [French Canadian rangers] worse than savages, are our allies, and their infamy soils our glory. . . . Such was the indignation felt by the regular French officers that they said they wished to ask to be allowed to carry on the war alone and refused as companions-in-arms the monsters capable of dishonouring us. "Heu fuge crudeles terras, fuge littus iniquum. [Alas! Flee from this cruel land, flee from the hostile shore.]"

It is not difficult to understand why the Governor had turned against Bougainville, the loyal friend and aide of Montcalm. Jealous of the latter's success, Vaudreuil now did his best to tarnish it, complaining that the General "had stopped half way on the road to success, and instead of following his instructions, had contented himself with one victory, when he should have gained two by capturing Fort Edward". Vaudreuil's criticism of Montcalm was based on the following facts. On the 8th, the day Munro signed the articles of capitulation, thousands of militia from neighbouring provinces had begun to pour in to reinforce Webb's garrison, but too late to come to the aid of the gallant old Scot Munro. Within a few days hundreds upon hundreds of men were bivouacked on the fields surrounding Fort Edward, doing nothing, disgusted and mutinous, declaring that they were ready to fight but not to lie about without tents, blankets or kettles. Webb wrote to Loudon on 14 August that most of those from New York had already deserted and had threatened to shoot their officers if they tried to stop them. A general mutiny, however, was aborted, but only after a sergeant had been shot and a number of militiamen arrested. Nevertheless, the greatest disorder reigned until the 17th, when Webb, learning that the

French had gone, ordered the discontented men back to their homes. Vaudreuil's contention was that Montcalm had here missed his great opportunity: had he marched immediately to Fort Edward he could, in the general confusion, have carried it by a *coup de main*. Well, perhaps it might just have been possible, but how much did Montcalm know of the confusion reigning at Fort Edward? Vaudreuil conveniently overlooked the fact that Montcalm had lost almost half his force when the Indians decamped after the massacre, and, moreover, that owing to the inefficiency (malversation perhaps would be a more appropriate word) of his friend Bigot's Commissary arrangements, the French army was short of supplies. He also overlooked the fact that he had ordered Montcalm, "as a matter of the greatest necessity", to see that the Canadians under the General's command should be returned to their homes *before* September, to gather in the crops. He certainly would have been the first to complain if his orders had not been obeyed. Lastly, since Montcalm had no transport by which to convey his cannon to Fort Edward, a siege would have been impossible.

Shortly after Bougainville's arrival in Montreal, the Indians who had left the army began to appear in the city, bringing with them about 200 prisoners. Vaudreuil merely rebuked them for breaking the terms of capitulation and then bought from them some of the prisoners, at the price of two kegs of brandy each, with the inevitable consequences.

> I thought [writes Bougainville] that the Governor would have told them they should have neither provisions nor presents until all the English were released; that he himself would have gone to their huts and taken the prisoners from them; and that the *habitants* would be forbidden under the severest penalties from selling, or giving them brandy. I saw the contrary, and I shuddered at the sight of what my eyes beheld. On the 15th, at two o'clock, in the presence of the whole town, they killed one of the prisoners, put him into a kettle and forced his wretched countrymen to eat him.

Bigot, the friend of Vaudreuil, confirms the story, while another French writer, whose diary fell into the hands of a British man o' war, relates that "the Indians compelled mothers to eat the flesh of their own children". Bigot declares that guns, canoes, and other presents were given to the western tribes by Vaudreuil before they left Montreal, on the principle that "They must be sent home satisfied at any cost."

> Such were the pains taken to preserve allies who were useful chiefly through the terror inspired by their diabolical cruelties. This time their cruelty cost them dear. They had dug up and scalped corpses in the

graveyard of Fort William Henry, many of which were remains of
victims of the small-pox; and the savages caught the disease, which
is said to have made great havoc among them.

Vaudreuil, in reporting to the Minister of Marine what he calls "*my* capture of
Fort William Henry", takes great credit for his "generous procedures" towards
the British prisoners, presumably alluding to the fact that he had bought some
of them from the Indians with brandy, which was certain to cause the death of
others.

"Such was Vaudreuil's obsequiousness to his red allies that he let them do
what they pleased", writes another French contemporary. "They were seen
roaming about Montreal, knife in hand, threatening everybody and often in-
sulting those they met. When complaint was made, he [the Governor] did
nothing. Far from it; instead of reproaching them, he loaded them with gifts,
in the belief that their cruelty would then relent." (Anon, *Mémories sur le Canada
1749–60*.)

After about a fortnight, nearly all the surviving prisoners had been ransomed; only then, after a final distribution of presents and a great drunken
debauch, did the whole savage troop at last consent to paddle home to their
villages in the west.

Once again winter set its icy grip on Canada and campaigning was confined to
partisan raids. On his return from Carillon Bougainville wrote to Mme Hérault,

Now, for the last time this year, *ma chère maman*, I have the chance to
chat to you. Already this unhappy country has been snowbound for a
week and soon the frosts will be added to the other hardships we must
expect in a winter of eight months' duration. During all that time I
shall be thinking of you and of France; I shall improve my mind and
let myself profit by the body's discomforts. On my return, *chère
maman*, you will perhaps find me rather peculiar, sometimes philo-
sophical, sometimes not, with the same passions as previously, but
with more frequent flashes of wisdom, a stronger tendency to think
plenty of fine ideas, but with no very great capacity for carrying them
out. What can you expect? These natural surroundings, so apt to
engender and maintain a melancholy temper, the moods which follow
one another, always sad and sometimes hideous—even horrifying;
the very nature of this cruel country, and yet still more the disposition
of those who live in it . . . what a field for misanthropy; what a setting
for regrets and fond desires. At the very thought of some day quitting
this exile, one's mood seems to brighten and cheerfulness revives, but

the illusion quickly fades and the present stern reality obliterates all that lies ahead for the future. That, *ma chère maman*, is your child's present condition—a sort of crisis which demands a stout heart [*qui exigerait une âme à plusieurs étages*]. The thought that you love me a little and that I must deserve your good opinion is the only thing that upholds me . . . whatever I do I imagine that you are with me and are here to be my judge, to condemn or approve. . . . I admit that your opinion of me will always be the true measure of my worth, and that should you cease to care for me my ambition would be snuffed out like a candle.

This winter of 1757–8, which Bougainville spent almost entirely in Quebec, passed almost without incident. Again there was a shortage of food. In Quebec and Montreal there were riots, and violent protests against the issue of horse-flesh in lieu of beef. A mob gathered before the Governor's house and a deputation of women beset him, crying out that the horse was the friend of man and that their religion forbade its consumption. In reply the Governor threatened them with imprisonment or hanging; but with little effect and the crowd dispersed, only to stir up the soldiers quartered in the town. The colonial regulars, ill disciplined at best, mutinied and stirred to join them a battalion of French regulars billeted in the town. Vaudreuil was powerless; Montcalm was in Quebec, and the task of dealing with the mutineers fell to the Chevalier de Lévis. Bougainville tells us that he proved equal to the crisis, taking a high tone, threatening death to the first soldiers who should refuse to eat horseflesh, assuring them that he himself ate it every day. "Thus," to quote Bougainville, "by a characteristic mingling of authority and tact, he quelled the storm."

The food shortage did not, however, affect what Montcalm ironically refers to as the "court". Bigot, at what was known as his "palace", continued to entertain twenty persons a day to dinner—at the King's expense. There was also a hall for dancing, but gambling was the chief feature of his entertainments, and the stakes grew higher and higher as the war went on. Bigot himself played desperately; early in 1758 he lost 204,000 francs—a loss which he well knew how to recoup. Francis Parkman writes,

> The chief Canadian families were so social in their habits and so connected by inter-marriage that, along with the French civil and military officers of the colonial establishment, they formed a society whose members all knew each other, like the corresponding English class in Virginia. There was among them a social facility and ease rare in democratic communities; and in the ladies of Quebec and Montreal there were often seen graces which visitors from France were astonished to find at the edge of the wilderness. Yet this small though lively society had anomalies which grew more obtrusive towards the close

of the war. Knavery makes strange companions; and at the tables of high officials and colony officers of rank sat guests as boorish in manners as they were worthless in character. (*Montcalm and Wolfe*, vol. II.)

One such was a notorious swindler named Cadet, a native of Bordeaux.

Montcalm, in his official capacity, was obliged not only to attend these functions, but also, much against his inclination, to entertain the "big-wigs" (*les grandes perruques*, the very words he uses in writing to his mother) himself. This was social duty that he could ill afford and that caused him to incur considerable debts. "How bored I am," he wrote to his mother, "how I wish I could return home. . . ." Bougainville too was obliged to attend these social functions, though it must be admitted that he enjoyed gambling and the sleigh-rides over the snow-covered icebound St Lawrence in the company of pretty women. But, as the interminable winter months dragged on, he too became bored and more and more appalled at the disgraceful misappropriation of public funds. In his "Mémoire sur les fraudes commises dans la colonie" (part of his *Mémoires sur l'état de la Nouvelle France*) he reveals the almost unbelievable extent to which peculation was practised; even the transportation of military stores gave an opportunity for plunder. As Bougainville was to find out, Montcalm's campaign against Fort William Henry had been delayed by three months solely because Cadet had bought up all the supplies of wheat, and then, when famine threatened, had then sold them at an exorbitant price. This is but one example. From the Commissary-General to Canadian military commanders of outlying forts, who falsified their accounts and sold to the Indians what had been intended as gifts from the King of France, peculation was rife. Francis Parkman comments,

> A contagion of knavery ran through the official life of the colony, and to resist it required no common share of robustness. The officers of the troops of the line [the *métropolitain*] were not much within its influence; but those of the militia and colony regulars, whether French or Canadian by birth, shared the corruption of the Civil Service. Seventeen of them, including six Chevaliers of the order of Saint-Louis and eight commandants of forts, were afterwards arraigned for fraud and malversation. . . .

"Not enough", Bougainville was to write, "to save Sodom."

It was thanks to a letter of 12 April 1759 written in cipher by Montcalm, with the help of Bougainville, and addressed to the Maréchal de Belle Isle, that these immense frauds were finally brought to light; but the day of final reckoning was yet to come. Even before this, however, the Minister of War had sent Vaudreuil and Bigot a despatch, dated 20 February 1759, that angered and humiliated them by ordering them and their entourage not to do anything without first consulting Montcalm, not only in matters of war, but also in all matters of administration touching the defence and preservation of the colony. In April the French Government sent an agent from Bordeaux to make an investigation. This astute man played the part of detective and wormed his way into the secrets of Bigot and his confederates. After six months of patient probing he tracked down four distinct combinations for public plunder. A terrified Bigot, hoping to exonerate himself, broke with Cadet and made him disgorge 2 million louis of stolen money. But the net was closing round the Commissary-General and his partners, who, in a vain effort to escape final retribution, gave up nearly 7 million livres more. Stormy events followed, and the culprits found shelter for a time amid the tumult of war. Peculation did not cease, but the day of reckoning was at hand.

On 22 February, Bougainville returned to Montreal, where he spent the rest of the winter season. Twice he visited his Iroquois "family" at Saut St Louis, bringing with him presents of tobacco and vermilion. His generosity was rewarded by his promotion, by election, from blood-brother to son of the tribe—a great honour. Henceforth he was to be considered a true child of the race, not just an honorary brother. His second visit to his "family" was not at all, however, so agreeable as his first, for on this second occasion he was obliged to participate in mourning ceremonies for some of his Iroquois "brothers" who had been killed in a skirmish with British troops. War was war, and these ritual ceremonies seemed ridiculous, if not downright offensive, to Bougainville. By all means honour the brave; but public mourning and false tears and moans— no. The smoking of the *calumet* (a tobacco pipe) at the burial had no appeal to our young *philosophe*.

On 19 May the year's first French warships and transports arrived at Quebec. The news they brought was bad: the French had lost the bloody battle of Rosbach against the King of Prussia. On learning the news, Bougainville was prompted to exclaim, "The tidings from Europe proves the truth of that Greek proverb which says, 'It is better to be an army of stags commanded by a lion, than an army of lions commanded by a stag!'"

At Leuthen, with a force of 30,000 Prussians, Frederick had, furthermore, achieved the near-impossible by defeating an army of 80,000 Austrians and driving them out of Silesia. But, while Britain's ally was reaping continental laurels, she herself, under the inept administration of Newcastle, had been suffering nothing but humiliation. Britain had lost Minorca (for which the innocent Byng had been shot); from America came news of Loudon's manifold failures; from Germany came news of the misfortunes of the Duke of Cumberland, who at the head of an army of Germans on British pay had been forced to sign the Convention of Kloster-Zeven, by which he promised to disband them; and, on top of all this a proposed attack on Rochefort had resulted in complete failure, owing to disagreement between the British naval and military commanders. (This last setback occurred during Pitt's first, short administration, of

1756–7, but the failure of the expedition cannot be blamed on him.) The unpopularity of the Government was further increased by the decision to post Hanoverian troops in England, against a hypothetical French invasion.

The French might well have thought that they had little to fear from Britain. The aged Lord Chesterfield wrote, "Whoever is in or out of office I am sure we are undone both at home and abroad: at home by our increasing debt and expenses; abroad by our ill-luck and incapacity. We are no longer a nation."

But now the miracle occurred. By popular acclaim William Pitt, the Great Commoner, was recalled to become Secretary of State and Leader of the House of Commons, with full control of the war and foreign affairs.

Chapter Five

The Third Campaign

Under Pitt's vigorous administration, Britain's war efforts were redoubled. The Great Commoner perceived the situation in Canada and New England much more clearly than his predecessors in office had done. It came as no secret to Montcalm that Britain was planning a simultaneous attack on Louisbourg, Carillon and Fort Duquesne and that massive reinforcements were on their way. Immediate action was essential, but the planning of the campaign was to cause further bitterness between Vaudreuil and the French commander. Despite this, on 13 June Montcalm arrived at Carillon, accompanied by Bougainville, who had been promoted to the rank of assistant quartermaster. A British force of some 13,000 men, commanded by General Abercromby, was preparing to attack the 3,500 men at Montcalm's disposal. The French general had established his position a little in advance of the fort, on a height buttressed by trunks of trees packed with turf. On his right was stationed the Chevalier de Lévis, on his left Colonel de Bourlamaque. The heat was overpowering. On 8 July, when the British advance guard emerged from the woods, Montcalm doffed his coat and, turning to his men, cried, "*Mes enfants*! This day will be a warm one."

The British, who were ordered by Abercromby to attack with the bayonet, advanced bravely against the French breastworks, but were no match for the extraordinarily accurate fire of the French and the few Canadians under de Lévis. Wave after wave advanced against the French, who, sheltered behind their stout wooden and turf parapets, shot them down before they could come to grips with them. Nevertheless, the British, including picked battalions of Highlanders (an innovation introduced by Pitt to ensure their loyalty—the Stuart rising of 1745 was, after all, not so far back in the past) continued to charge fearlessly, until suddenly, from the extreme right, came the cry, "En avant, les Canadiens!" The Chevalier de Lévis had judged the moment propitious to order a sortie by his Canadian rangers. Despite a last desperate rally, the British fell back in disorder, leaving thousands of casualties on the field. Of the French officers, fourteen were killed and twenty wounded. Of the French colonial companies, only two officers were wounded and twenty-one men killed or wounded. Bougainville received a slight head wound, which rendered him temporarily unconscious. As he was being carried from the field for dead, he recovered his senses and protested that his place was beside his general and continued to fight. Bourlamaque, however, was severely wounded and was forced to retire. De Lévis, who was shot at twice, miraculously escaped unhurt.

If young Lord Howe, originally appointed to command the expedition, had not been killed while leading a reconnaissance party, the outcome of the battle might have been very different. The death of this gallant officer on the very eve of the engagement with the French, was an incalculable loss to the British. Wolfe described Howe as "the noblest Englishman that has appeared in my time and the best soldier in the British army". Pitt calls him "a character of ancient times; a complete model of military virtue". This young nobleman (he was only thirty-four) had all the qualities of a leader of men. From general to drummer boy, all in the British forces loved and esteemed him. Over the past year he had studied the art of forest warfare. Sharing all the hardships of his men (even cooking for himself), he had introduced reforms that entirely broke with the traditions of the regular army. He made his men throw off all useless encumbrances and wear their hair short; had them wear leather leggings instead of stockings or cloth gaiters, so as to protect their legs from thorns; and ordered them to cut off their coat-tails, to brown the barrels of their muskets and to carry in their knapsacks thirty pounds of meal, to cook for themselves. An admiring Frenchman wrote that these men could live for a month without their supply trains.

Major Mante, an English contemporary, wrote, "With the death of Lord Howe the soul of General Abercromby's army seemed to expire. From the unhappy moment when the General was deprived of his advice, neither order nor discipline was observed and a strange kind of infatuation usurped the place of resolution. The death of one man was the ruin of 15,000." (*Sic.* Major Marte's figure.)

In this necessarily very abridged account of the battle that followed Howe's death, I have been unable to enter into many details of the action itself, of Abercromby's incompetence when he assumed command, or of his pusillanimous behaviour later, of which Montcalm took every advantage. Abercromby was not on the scene of the battle, but a mile and a half distant. He was unable to prevent the panic-stricken retreat of his army back to their camp, even though he had reserves in plenty; and he need not have allowed quantities of military equipment and stores to fall into the hands of the French.

On the morning of 12 July the Hymn of Victory was chanted by the whole French army. By Montcalm's orders a great cross was raised on the site, bearing an inscription that he had himself composed:

Quid dux? Quid miles? Quid ingentia ligna?
En signum! En victor! Deus hic, Deus ipse triumphat!
Chrétien, ce ne fut point Montcalm et sa prudence,
Ces arbres renversés, ces héros, leurs exploits,

Qui des Anglais confus ont brisé l'espérance;
C'est le bras de ton Dieu vainqueur sur cette croix.

(What leader? What soldier? What mighty timbers?
See the sign! See the victor! God himself here triumphs!
Christian, it was not Montcalm and his prudence,
These fallen trees, these heroes, their exploits
Who destroyed the hope of the confused English;
It was the arm of your conquering God on this Cross.)

As soon as Bougainville had recovered from his wound, Montcalm sent him to Montreal to report on the situation to Vaudreuil. This time Vaudreuil really surpassed himself in petty jealousy, more especially as the victory had been won thanks to French troops of the line with no help from Indians and very little from Canadians: when de Lévis ordered his rangers to charge the British, the British were already demoralized and the battle was virtually already won. In a letter to the Colonial Minister, Vaudreuil declared that "the victory would have bad results" (though he gives no hint of what these might be); that Montcalm had mismanaged the whole affair; that "he would have been beaten but for 'the manifest interposition of Heaven'"; and, finally, that he had failed to follow his (Vaudreuil's) instructions, though he neglected to state that his instructions had been to avoid a general engagement. There followed the most acrimonious correspondence. Vaudreuil even went so far as to write to the Minister of Marine,

> As the King has entrusted this colony to me, I cannot help warning you of the unhappy consequences should the Marquis de Montcalm remain here. I shall keep him by me until I receive your orders. It is essential that they reach me early. I pass over in silence all the infamous conduct and indecent talk he has held or countenanced; but I should be wanting in my duty to the King if I did not beg you to ask for his recall.

In criticizing Montcalm for not following up the British defeat by driving the enemy back to the Hudson, Vaudreuil quite overlooked the fact that his promised reinforcements did not arrive until after the engagement; that the French lines of communication were stretched to the limit; and that, as usual, the French forces were short of supplies—indeed, had only eight days' rations left. Abercromby, however, though he had shown himself an abject poltroon, had reserves in plenty.

Bougainville bravely defended his general. In the three campaigns in which he had taken part, Montcalm had been three times victorious.

Now at last the war is being conducted on the European model. There are plans of campaign, there are arms, artillery, sieges and battles. It is no longer a question of dealing a single blow, but of conquering or being conquered. What a revolution! What a change! One might have thought that the people of this country, overwhelmed by the novelty of everything, would have had time to accustom themselves to the new state of affairs, and more time still to reflect on what they had seen; and even more time to efface those earlier ideas which by now have hardened into dangerous, childish prejudices; and, finally, even more time still to master the underlying causes, to draw conclusions and submit at last to the wisdom of experience. On the contrary, townsfolk, financiers, business men, officers, bishops, vicars, Jesuits, one and all prophesy, criticize, expound, never stop talking or dissertating on the war. Everyone thinks himself a Turenne. . . . What a tragedy for this country, which will fall a victim either to its prejudices or to the knavery of its leaders.

On 13 August Bougainville returned to Carillon and on the following day was ordered to the camp of the humiliated British to negotiate several outstanding questions. There he was received with the greatest courtesy. Among the British officers were old acquaintances from his diplomatic days in London, including Captain Abercromby, nephew of the General, with whom he wagered a case of champagne that the British would never capture the fortress of Louisbourg. A week later, he learnt that he had lost his wager. The British amphibious operation under the command of General Amherst and Admiral Boscawen had been carried out in appalling weather, with the surf so high and a swell so heavy, often with the additional hazards of fog and gales, that any landing seemed out of the question. Some boats were stove in on the rocks, others overset, thereby drowning soldiers, sailors, guns and stores. But, miraculously, either by a deliberate misunderstanding of orders, or by sheer bloody-mindedness, the first boats reached the storm-lashed beach, under command of two young lieutenants and an ensign. Wolfe, already a sick man, second-in-command to General Amherst, immediately followed, armed only with a cane, and, under a withering fire from concealed French batteries, established a bridgehead. The whole operation seemed an act of madness. None of the siege guns could be got ashore until the 18th, and more than a hundred boats were stove in.

The bravery of both British and French in attack and defence can scarcely be paralleled. But, once the British guns had been positioned to bombard the town, and Admiral Boscawen's ships were able to add their fire-power to that of the army's, the town was reduced to rubble, except for the citadel, though even this was reduced to a mere shell. On 27 July the French were obliged to capitulate. The French commander, Drucour, and his garrison had made a gallant defence. It had been his aim to prolong the siege until it should be too late for

Amherst to co-operate with Abercromby in an attack on Canada, and in this at
least he had succeeded. 5,637 French officers, soldiers and sailors were taken
prisoner. Eighteen mortars and 221 canon and a great quantity of arms, ammunition and stores fell into the hands of the British. Such of the prisoners not dis-
abled by wounds or sickness were embarked for Britain; the merchants and
inhabitants of Louisbourg were sent to France. Brigadier Whitmore, appointed
governor of the ruined town, remained with four regiments to hold guard over
the desolation they had made.

Bougainville delivered his case of champagne to Captain Abercromby with
a heavy heart.

On 9 September, Bougainville returned to Montreal with Montcalm. The
situation there was desperate: food prices had risen to such giddy heights that
officers were unable to live on their pay. "Everyone sees how it is", wrote
Bougainville, "and everyone knows what is wrong and complaint is universal,
but what does that matter to the extortionists who abuse their authority?"

Montcalm, despite his last victory and probably his most brilliant, could
foresee no hope for a colony so maladministered, so short of military personnel
and invariably so lacking in provisions. Early in September his worst fears were
realized. Fort Frontenac, which controlled Lake Ontario, had baffled Shirley's
attempt to reduce Niagara and given Montcalm the opportunity to capture
Oswego, had been captured by a small force of 3,000 provincials under Lieutenant-Colonel Bradstreet. On 26 September, de Noyan, the French commandant,
surrendered himself and his garrison, which consisted of only 110 soldiers and
some labourers recruited from among prisoners of war. Bradstreet captured
nine armed vessels (the whole French naval force of Lake Ontario) and an enor-
mous quantity of war material. The French command of Lake Ontario was
now lost. Fort Duquesne was the next to fall, for the greater part of the garrison
had earlier deserted or retired, owing to the lack of provisions, and the few
troops remaining were unable to withstand the shock of the British attack.
Moreover, some of the Canadians had mutinied, while the Indian allies heartily
disliked the commandant, de Ligneris, who was drunk every day. Not only
were they unprepared to accept his orders, but many of them deserted to the
British. Louisiana was henceforth cut off from Canada.

The Canadian *habitants*, hitherto lulled into a false sense of security by
Vaudreuil's boastful and lying reports, at last woke up to the seriousness of the
situation. Someone with the voice of authority must go and seek support from
the Court of France. Even Vaudreuil recognized that this was essential and for
once was in agreement with Montcalm (though with reservations, as we shall
see) that the man for the job was Bougainville, supported by Doreil.

Chapter Six

Bougainville's Mission to the French Court

On 3 November, Bougainville left Montreal in a vessel carrying five British officers to Quebec. Doriel travelled separately, to ensure that at least one of the two emissaries should arrive safely on the shores of France. The first stage of the journey almost ended in disaster, for Bougainville's boat was wrecked and he and the five British officers spent the night on a rock only six feet above water-level. At daybreak they swam through icy waters to the shore, over a mile distant. Bougainville has little to say about this exploit except to repeat his usual plaint: "What a country! What a journey! Better a civilian than have to suffer this sort of thing!"

What is interesting is that this gallant soldier should ever have become one of the world's most famous mariners and navigators, since the rest of the journey in a St Malo privateer, the *Victoire*, was terrible. Tossed about by mountainous seas, the ship was twice on the point of foundering. Twice the crew vowed that wherever the ship first touched land they would have a solemn mass celebrated and walk in procession barefoot to the nearest church to give thanksgiving to God for their safe arrival. It is unlikely that these hardy Breton sailors were aware that Columbus's crew had made the same vow almost 300 years previously.

Bougainville, who even in the most abject straits of adversity could never forget his classical education, wrote, "I could almost feel tempted to forgive Aeneas the tears he shed when storms were blowing. One may be a hero, yet afraid to be drowned.... Oh! far, far happier to be a gardener planting cabbages, for at least he has one foot on the ground and the other close to it on the shoulder of his spade!"

As though the appalling crossing were not enough, the ship's compass proved defective, and, instead of sailing into St Malo, they found themselves in the Bristol Channel. Fortunately they recognized their navigational error in time, and successfully avoided interception by British cruisers. On 20 December Bougainville was in Paris. However intoxicating it may have been for the young aide-de-camp to be once again in the atmosphere of his beloved Paris and to see once more his dear *maman*, he fully realized his tremendous responsibilities, and, as soon as rested, devoted himself to work.

Vaudreuil had given him a laudatory letter of introduction to the Colonial Minister: "He is better fitted in all respects than any other to inform you of the state of the colony. I have given him my instructions and you can trust entirely in what he tells you." Concerning Doreil he wrote to the Minister of War, "I have full confidence in him and he may be entirely trusted. Everybody here likes him." This was all very well, but with these introductions he also sent a private covering letter to his patron, in which he wrote, "In order to condescend to the wishes of M. de Montcalm and leave no means untried to keep in harmony with him, I have given letters to Messrs Doreil and Bougainville; but I have the honour to inform you, Monseigneur, that they do not understand the colony, and to warn you that they are the creatures of M. de Montcalm."

Bougainville obtained interviews with all the ministers concerned and, most important of all, with the Marquise de Pompadour, whom he succeeded in propitiating, though not, it seems, without difficulty and delay. But once in her presence he disclosed to her, as he had done to the Ministers of War, Marine and Colonies, the desperate state of Canada and the remedies that M. de Montcalm and he had devised to save it. He pointed out that the British were masters of 350 leagues of coastline, at any given point of which assistance from Britain could reach them. In the spring they would be able to muster close on 80,000 well-equipped men under arms. On the other hand, as he pointed out, the French, with 3,400 regulars, 1,200 marines and about 6,000 (unreliable) militiamen, were so lacking in all *matériel*, even gunpowder, that, should the British reach Quebec, there would not be enough in reserve to keep the guns in action for more than six days. A naval force must be sent to protect the mouth of the St Lawrence, and reinforcements of at least 1,500 infantry, besides engineers, gunners and artillery. Bougainville pointed out that, while formerly the British colonists had been split by political and religious principles, now, with the exception of the Pennsylvanians, whose Quaker religious tenets forbade them to participate in war, they were unanimous in their determination to oust the French and in their support for the British Crown. If the necessary French reinforcements were forthcoming, it would be possible, by disembarking 4,000 men on the coast of Carolina, to create a diversion that would liberate New France from impossibly heavy pressure.

Madame de Pompadour listened sympathetically to all that Bougainville told and promised to use all her influence in his support.

The idea of a landing in Carolina seemed to her to be excellent. Without delay she submitted the plan to a council of ministers, by whom it was approved, though funds necessary for its implementation were still to be found. Unfortunately the royal treasury was empty and, although Madame de Pompadour tried to raise the necessary 2 million livres, the fruitless European war had swallowed up everything. The constant changes of ministers and generals made consistency of policy difficult, if not impossible. D'Argenson was succeeded as Minister of

War by Belle Isle; Richelieu by Soubise; Bernis, Minister of Foreign Affairs, by Choiseul; Moras, Minister of Marine, by Berryer.

Bougainville acquitted himself of his mission with all the zeal and loyalty expected of him. He had no hesitation in informing the ministers concerned of the shameful thieving and scandalous peculation practised by the Canadian administration. He described the danger to the colony caused by the dissensions dividing Montcalm, Vaudreuil and the Commissary. He emphasized the fact that the subordination of Montcalm to the Governor paralysed the General's movements and that Montcalm was the only military man on the spot capable of saving Canada. Berryer, as Minister of Marine, was convinced. He wrote to the Commissary,

> It is His Majesty's intention that M. le Marquis de Montcalm shall be consulted not only upon all operations of a military nature, but also on all matters having a bearing upon the defence and safekeeping of the colony. You will take counsel with him on the contents of such letters as I may write to you relative to that subject and you will conduct your dealings with him in such a manner as to win his confidence, as he on his side will endeavour to merit yours. You should never lose sight of the necessity for this close co-operation—more than ever now that the salvation of the colony depends upon it; and that the King desires it above all else.

Berryer wrote in the same strain to Vaudreuil:

> It remains to me to impress upon you the importance of remaining in perfect agreement with M. de Montcalm and of forgetting the petty differences of opinion which may have formerly existed between you. . . . You yourself should not take part in any campaign unless it be of a nature so decisive that you find yourself obliged, for the general defence of the colony, to place in action all the militia of the country. Short of a crisis of this gravity, you should remain at the administrative centre of the colony, and so be in a condition to keep watch on all that passes.

This certainly seemed a victory for Bougainville, but Berryer was in fact already prepossessed against the young aide-de-camp by Vaudreuil's secret warning, and in reply to the young man's reiterated appeals for military help he tartly answered, "Eh, Monsieur, when the house is on fire, one cannot occupy oneself with the stable." To which Bougainville impertinently replied, "At least, Monsieur, nobody will be able to say that you talk like a horse." Belle Isle wrote to Montcalm to the effect that it was necessary to concentrate all the strength of the kingdom for a decisive operation in Europe and that therefore the required aid could not be sent, and that the King entrusted everything to Montcalm's zeal and generalship, joined with the valour of the victors of Ticonderoga. All that could be spared was 300–400 recruits for regulars, and sixty engineers, sappers and artillerymen, along with gunpowder, arms and provisions. It was said that these men and supplies (together with those brought over by the contractor Cadet) would be sufficient to carry the colony through the next campaign!

Parsimonious as was this assistance, Bougainville's mission had not been entirely wasted. "To him who has nothing, even a little counts", wrote Montcalm to Berryer. Bougainville had also been successful in weeding out the administration and putting a check on waste. The results of his mission were to have a great effect on morale in Canada.

Towards the end of February 1759, Bougainville made his respectful adieux to the Court of Versailles, and took ship from Bordeaux for Quebec. Prior to his departure he drew up and addressed to Montcalm a curious message in cipher summing up the results of his embassy and of his two-month visit to France. He begins,

> For your eye alone:
> The embodiment of the militia approved and recommended. . . .
> Plan of retreat to Louisiana thought well of, but not accepted. Project
> against Carolina approved but not followed up, for lack of funds. The
> magic of the savages, their character, that of the Canadians, the gross
> jealousies, self-interest, knavery, enlarged upon; the court furious at
> the expenditure; strong letter to M. Bigot. M. de Vaudreuil lacking
> talent, but will be supported by the Navy; [he thinks he] owes you
> the Grand Cross of St Louis, which I asked for him in your name, thus
> doing you both honour and gilding the pill. Fight to the finish but if
> you do not lose all, aspire to all. You are the man of the day. . . . The
> King a mere cipher—Madame la Marquise all powerful. Prime
> Minister had been informed you were too hasty; to my credit I
> destroyed that impression. The Duc de Choiseul your friend. M.
> Berryer upright but hard, good-natured. The Prince de Conti, no
> authority, furious. M. le Comte d'Argenson, M. le Marquis de
> Paulmy fallen from power. The Jesuits in a more critical position than
> ever. Wherever you look a lack of stability both in the council chamber and in the public forum. Credit, none. In the Exchequer everything left to chance. . . . In short if you do not lose all, you will gain a
> triumph. You have no enemy, nor even a rival to grudge it to you.
> Were I to mention all the persons who like you and who would wish
> to see you a Marshal of France, I should have to name the whole
> country. Little children speak your name. . . .

In his strange cipher letter Bougainville neglects to mention that he had several times been received in audience by the King, who, although sympathetic to the young man's demands, was powerless to help. It was small consolation that His Most Christian Majesty promoted the young emissary from Canada to the rank of colonel and made him a Chevalier of Saint Louis; that de Bourlamaque was honoured in the same way; and that Montcalm was made a lieutenant-general and de Lévis a major-general (added to which, Vaudreuil was presented with the Grand Cross of Saint Louis). It was men and supplies that Bougainville had come for, not rank and honour. But, as Maurice Thiéry writes, "Avocat, mathématicien, homme du monde et homme de guerre, Bougainville s'était révélé une étoile de première grandeur dans le firmament de la diplomatie." ("Lawyer, mathematician, soldier, courtier, Bougainville stood revealed as a star of the first magnitude in the firmament of diplomacy.")

C

Chapter Seven

British Preparations for the Final Assault—
The Plains of Abraham

On 10 May 1759, Bougainville sailed up the St Lawrence. With him came a squadron bearing the supplies and the paltry reinforcements so grudgingly provided. In a pessimistic despatch from the Maréchal de Belle Isle, Minister of War, Montcalm was told what was expected of him and why he and the colony were abandoned to their fate:

> If we sent a large consignment of troops, there would be a great fear that the English would intercept them on the way; and as the King could never send you forces equal to those which the English are prepared to oppose to you, the effect would have no other consequence than to excite the Cabinet in London to increased efforts for preserving its superiority on the American continent.
>
> As we must expect the English to turn all their force against Canada and attack you on several sides at once, it is necessary that you limit your plans of defence to the most essential points and those most closely connected, so that being concentrated within a smaller space each part may be within easy reach of support and help from the rest. However small may be the space you are able to hold, it is indispensable to keep a footing in North America, for if we once lose the country entirely its recovery will be almost impossible. The King counts on your zeal, courage and persistency to accomplish this object and relies on you to spare no pains and no exertions. Impart this resolution to your chief officers and join with them to inspire your soldiers with it. I have answered for you to the King; I am confident that you will not disappoint me . . . and that you will go to the greatest extremity rather than submit to conditions as shameful as those imposed at Louisbourg, the memory of which you will wipe out.

To this Montcalm answered, "We shall save this unhappy colony or perish."

Although there was still a great disparity of numbers between the opposing forces—the British could raise at least 50,000 men, while Vaudreuil's estimate of effectives, including French regulars, militia, *courreurs de bois* and perhaps 2,000 Indians, amounted to only just over 15,000—there was good hope that the centre of the colony could still be defended; for the only avenues by which the British could approach the interior were barred by the rock of Quebec, the rapids of the St Lawrence, and the strongpoint of Île-aux-Noix, at the outlet of Lake Champlain. Should every effort of resistance fail and the British force their way into the heart of Canada, Montcalm proposed, as a last desperate resort, to abandon the valley of the St Lawrence and descend the Mississippi with as many of his troops and *habitants* as possible and make a last stand among the swamps and marshes of Louisiana.

Vaudreuil, naturally, disagreed with Belle Isle's proposals (similar to those made by Bougainville and Montcalm) to concentrate the French forces, but stated that, should the British indeed penetrate as far as Quebec, he himself would take command of the army and militia and, if defeated there, would contain the enemy at Carillon. In the event he was to do neither. His official exclusion from all interference in the command of the army tended only to worsen his relations with Montcalm, de Lévis, de Bourlamaque and, at least temporarily, Bougainville—though he was forced to concede that in the circumstances the young colonel had in some respects succeeded quite well in his mission to Paris. But, in addition to the news, galling to Vaudreuil, that the Governor had been deprived of virtually all military command, Bougainville brought confirmation that three British fleets, consisting of twenty-two ships of the line, with frigates, sloops and a great number of transports, were concentrating at Louisbourg for an attack on Quebec. With these ships had come 9,000 men, commanded by the thirty-two-year-old General James Wolfe. On 6 June 1759, the last ship of the British fleet sailed out of Louisbourg harbour, the troops cheering and the officers drinking the toast, "British colours on every French fort, port and garrison in America."

Even before the British fleet had consolidated, Bougainville was making preparations to establish camps along the St Lawrence. It was decided that Montcalm should set up his headquarters on the plateau dominating the riverbank at Beauport (some distance downstream from Quebec), where he would have Bougainville's camp on his right, and on his left, extending as far as the Montmorency river, that of the Chevalier de Lévis. From these points they could not only keep watch on the enemy movements should they dare to move up the St Lawrence and make a landing, but at the same time keep in constant touch with each other. Nobody, not even Wolfe, or for that matter Amherst, nor indeed Montcalm or Bougainville and the former's second-in-command could imagine a direct assault on Quebec up the so-called heights of Abraham—something which is now familiar to every schoolboy or girl.

The great battle of the Plains of Abraham, as it was to be called, did not—despite the schoolboy history books with their stories of Wolfe quoting Grey's

Elegy before dying and the heroism of the mortally wounded Montcalm—constitute the end of the Anglo-French War in America. The surrender of Quebec was by no means merely a matter of gallant highlanders clambering up precipitous cliffs and defeating a French army and then occupying a French Canadian city almost by surprise. No: the whole story is quite different. To begin with, on the 26th June, the British fleet commanded by Admiral Sir Charles Saunders (22 vessels of the line and 5 frigates) came into sight and disembarked troops on the island of Orléans. A further landing of British troops took place on a small peninsula on the right bank of the St Lawrence, known as Lévis Point. Wolfe established his headquarters on the left bank of the river alongside the position occupied by De Lévis, from which he was separated only by the narrow stream of the Montmorency river. Wolfe, whose only orders from Pitt had been "Quebec must be taken", had seen at once that the task would be of the greatest difficulty, and that to overcome the city's natural defences, apart from the tactical dispositions and entrenchments made by the French, would require little short of a miracle.

As soon as the British had consolidated their positions they began a systematic bombardment of the city, almost without break. At the same time, on the south bank of the river, detachments of pro-British American rangers—not Indians—were, to Wolfe's utter disgust, robbing, burning, scalping, raping and committing every sort of atrocity on innocent French civilians.

Wolfe, hoping to put a speedy end to operations, decided on an attack on de Lévis's camp under cover of the fleet. But de Lévis had his eyes open, and, even before the British troops, commanded by Generals Townshend and Murray, had entered into action, they were driven back across the river. A terrific storm now broke out. Wolfe ordered a general retreat. The French victory of Montmorency cost the English 433 men; the French, seventy.

It was then decided that Admiral Saunders, commander of the fleet, should seek to push his vessels up the St Lawrence to beyond Quebec, in order to cut off the French supplies lying in the storehouses and magazines about forty miles or so beyond the town. Little did Bougainville know that the boatswain of one of the boats that glided by so silently in the night was a certain James Cook, who too was to circumnavigate the globe.

Part of Admiral Saunders's fleet succeeded in running the gauntlet of Quebec, and, despite the fact that the St Lawrence there is barely a quarter of a league wide, the faulty aim of the French gunners ensured that none of the vessels was hit. The advance of the British vessels up-river constituted a grave menace, and to prevent a landing both banks of the river had to be protected, from Quebec to as far upstream as the river Jacques Cartier. Bougainville was detached from his post at Beauport and detailed to guard the river; Vaudreuil undertook personal command of Bougainville's former station. The young Colonel was faced with a most difficult and unrewarding task: together with the few reinforcements that reached him from time to time, he had just 350 men scattered along the river and a flying detachment of 1,100 grenadiers and volunteers of the battalions sent from France. The role of this detachment was to rush to the defence of any place threatened. On 8 August the British landed 1,500 men at Pointe-aux-Trembles. With a force of 300 soldiers and cavalry, Bougainville drove them back, killing or wounding 300.

"I need not remind you Monsieur", the Marquis de Vaudreuil wrote to him, "that the safety of the colony lies in your hands, since it is most certainly the plan of the enemy to cut our communications by making a landing in the north; and only the greatest vigilance will prevent him from so doing."

This was a completely unnecessary reminder. No one could have been more conscious than Bougainville of the importance of the task imposed upon him. Every day he rode up and down the banks of the river, sometimes fourteen leagues a day; and at night he often lay out under the stars, fully clothed and only half asleep, straining his ears for the slightest sound.

Bougainville was a tireless writer. He wrote note after note to Montcalm, to Vaudreuil and to his fellow officers, telling them of his impressions or asking their advice. He even wrote to officers in the British camp, gentlemen with whom he had made friends while he was employed as secretary to de Mirepoix in London. In fact, he kept up a regular correspondence with Captain Abercromby, with whom, it will be recollected, he had made and lost the bet of a case of champagne over the taking of Louisbourg. He even sent him French wine, in exchange for Bristol beer. "It is necessary in this barbarous country", he wrote, "to show as much politeness and humanity as possible, even to those with whom we are at war." He also kept up a most cordial relationship with General Townshend, with whose family he had been acquainted while in London. "It will always be my pleasure", wrote the General, "to justify as far as I myself am concerned the kindly feelings you seem to cherish towards my family."

By September Quebec was in ruins. Fort Niagara had fallen. Provisions were becoming more and more scarce and Canadian soldiers were deserting by hundreds to return to their farms. Montcalm and Bougainville were obliged to concentrate on restoring courage to the disheartened. Wolfe, in turn, began to despair of ever capturing Quebec. He wrote to Pitt, "Without the consolation of having rendered to the State any service worth the name, and with no prospect of doing so, my constitution is entirely ruined." Bougainville kept an uninterrupted watch to see that French boats, under cover of darkness, could still descend the river unmolested, bringing the shattered town and its defenders essential supplies. Wolfe's estimate of the situation was not far wrong. Quebec was a natural, seemingly impregnable fortress. Not 4,000 men, but four times 4,000 now stood in its defence, and their chiefs wisely resolved not to throw away the advantages of their position. Nothing more was heard of Vaudreuil's bold plan of attacking the invaders at their landing; and Montcalm had declared, in his usual erudite classical manner, that he would play the part not of Hannibal but of Fabius. His plan was to avoid a general battle, run no risks and protract the defence till the resources of the enemy were exhausted, or until the approaching winter forced them to withdraw. However, there yet remained one sure means of success to Wolfe. Amherst was moving, with a larger force than that possessed by Wolfe, against Ticonderoga. Should he capture it and advance into the colony, Montcalm would be forced to weaken his army by sending strong detachments to oppose him. Indeed, this seemed to be Wolfe's last hope—until a sudden terrific storm scattered and destroyed most of the ships carrying Amherst's troops. On the other hand, however, on two occasions French fire-ships sent against the British failed dismally in their mission and destroyed more of their own vessels than of those of the enemy.

As winter approached, Wolfe had not yet succeeded in gaining a footing on the northern bank of the river. The French army regained confidence, and there were optimistic hopes that the British army would withdraw before the winter season. The campaign so far had been indecisive and, although Quebec lay in ruins and the country along the right shore of the river had been devastated, the French army was still intact. Wolfe, the beloved of his troops, the ugly little ailing general, had no wish to return to Britain with bowed head, a failure. He became convinced, writes his French biographer, Maurice Thiéry, that

> Something difficult, mad, rash, must be attempted, something that prudence would condemn as unachievable, but with British daring might be ventured and perhaps succeed. With the approval of his generals, Wolfe planned to send 4,500 men down the river to the creek of Foulon, a small bay commanded by the Heights of Abraham, lying about a mile upstream from Quebec, on that reach of the river entrusted to the care of Bougainville. The enterprise, however, seemed doomed to failure in advance, for a landing here could hardly fail to alarm the French outposts and Bougainville with his flying column, while the troops from the various garrisons in the neighbourhood would have no difficulty in repelling all invaders. And yet an almost incredible chance brought about the complete success of the operation.

On the morning of 12 September, the contractor Cadet had requested from Bougainville permission for the departure on the night of 12–13 September of a convoy of boats loaded with flour. The advance posts stationed on the riverbanks had been warned and had received orders to allow the convoy to pass.

What Bougainville, then stationed at Cap Rouge, three leagues from Quebec, did not know was that the consignment of flour was postponed; so when, on the night of 12 September, he caught in the gloom a glimpse of men o' war and barges moving up the river, he took no action. Before long there remained only a single vessel mysteriously riding at anchor before Cap Rouge. Bougainville remained where he was, uneasy and perplexed. For some days past the British had been carrying out the most puzzling manoeuvres, their vessels moving up and down the river in all directions. "The behaviour of the enemy is indeed as disconcerting as it is ambiguous", Montcalm had written to the young colonel. Yet disconcerting and ambiguous as it was, no one anticipated a landing hard by the city. Montcalm and Vaudreuil had many times warned Bougainville always to keep up-river, repeatedly assuring him that no enemy landing of any consequence could take place except at St Augustin or at Point-aux-Trembles, four or seven leagues from Quebec. This reasoning seemed to Bougainville sound enough, but he nevertheless scanned anxiously the unidentified man o' war which lay hove-to in midstream before his position.

The barges that he had taken to be those despatched by Cadet turned on their course at about two o'clock in the morning and began drifting downstream in the direction of Quebec. When they were challenged by the guards on the heights of Samos and Sillery, a Scottish officer who spoke French answered quietly, "France. Convoy of supplies. Do not make a noise, or the English will hear us." Meanwhile a feint attack was made below the town. The thunder of the guns of Saunders's flotilla, the sky alight with incendiaries, and the shouts of command of British officers all led the French to believe that a major landing was to be attempted at the very gates of the city. Swiftly the current bore the British flotilla to a point just below the creek of Foulon. It was there, Wolfe had learned from an escaped prisoner, that a single steep path led to the top of the cliff at a point where lay a small outpost set by Bougainville. In the silence of the night twenty-seven British grenadiers, all volunteers, leapt ashore and clambered up the slope. There was not one French regular soldier to raise the alarm. Vergor, the commander of the small Canadian detachment stationed on the heights, was sleeping peacefully. A few Canadians, taking alarm, fired a volley and took to their heels. Vergor was wounded and taken prisoner. The grenadiers fired two flares as indication of their success. Wolfe, from the flagship *Sutherland*, now issued his last general orders. Seated with him in his cabin was his old school-fellow John Jervis, afterwards Lord St Vincent. Wolfe told him that he expected to die in battle the next day, and, taking from his bosom a miniature of Miss Lowther, his betrothed, gave it to Jervis asking him to return it to her if the presentiment should prove true.

For a full two hours the procession of boats, borne on the current, steered silently down the St Lawrence. The stars were visible, but the night was moonless and sufficiently dark. Wolfe was in one of the foremost boats; near him sat a young midshipman, John Robinson, later to be professor of natural philosophy at the University of Edinburgh, who in later life used to tell how Wolfe, in a low voice, repeated Gray's *Elegy in a Country Churchyard* to the officers about him, probably to relieve the strain of his own thoughts. It will be recollected that the poem contains the famous line, "The paths of Glory lead but to the grave."

"Gentlemen," said Wolfe, as his recital ended, "I would rather have written those lines than take Quebec."

Bougainville, stationed up-river at Cap Rouge, had no idea of what was happening. He did not know that the flour convoy had not sailed. He was deceived by the false bombardment of Quebec by the British fleet. It was not until nine o'clock on the following morning that he learned that 4,500 of Wolfe's troops were drawn up in line on the Plains of Abraham (a pastureland named after Martin Abraham, a Canadian pilot turned farmer), ready to confront the 5,000 men of Montcalm.

No sooner had he learned the incredible news than in utmost haste he gathered together all his available troops and set out for the scene of battle. It was almost midday before he arrived, and too late. A scene of appalling disaster met his eyes.

The French army, although taken by surprise, had succeeded in fronting the enemy and engaging in battle, but by this time was in full retreat before the victorious British. Bougainville succeeded only in covering the retreat.

The news reached him that General Wolfe had breathed his last and that his commander and close friend, Montcalm, was mortally wounded, with only twenty-four hours to live. "All the better," said Montcalm, when informed of the fact by his doctor, "for I shall not see the British in Quebec."

On the following day, when Bougainville learned of the death of the hero whom he had loved like a father, he cried, "My heart is wounded to its tenderest depths. Monsieur le Marquis de Montcalm fought a campaign worthy of Turenne himself and his death is our supreme misfortune."

Chapter Eight

Final Capitulation of Quebec and Montreal— Canada Ceded to the British

If only de Lévis had been in Quebec instead of in Montreal at the time of the battle, the situation might have been very different. The death of Montcalm seems to have entirely demoralized the Governor. Quebec had not yet fallen and the British were too weak to follow up their success in the field. Nevertheless, Vaudreuil had ordered a general retreat as far as the Jacques Cartier river. The camp at Beauport, which had served as Montcalm's headquarters, had been abandoned in the most appalling disorder. The garrison of Quebec, deprived of competent leadership, became so completely demoralized that the commandant, Monsieur de Ramezai (a gentleman of Jacobite descent, whose family name was in fact Ramsay), declared that famine, the number of deserters and the general devastation left him no other course but to surrender. The only sensible act performed by Vaudreuil was to summon de Lévis to his quarters on the Jacques Cartier river. The arrival of this thirty-nine-year-old future Marshal banished discouragement and revived faltering energies among both officers and men. "Forward!" he had cried. "This is no time to think of flight. Forward, every man, to the relief of Quebec. Because we have lost one battle it does not mean we have lost a colony."

Bougainville heard de Lévis's orders with greatest relief. Now, filled with new hope, he took the road to Quebec with a picked body of men, but within only a few miles of his objective he learned, to his consternation, that the exhausted city had surrendered to the British. Although de Lévis responded immediately and with all the vigour at his disposal, and although Bougainville and Bourlamaque held their ground, Ramezai had already raised the flag of surrender. De Lévis countermanded the order to surrender, but the Canadian militia refused to fight on—despite the fact that Bougainville had managed, by means of a hundred swift horsemen each carrying a sack of biscuits, to get some supplies into the beleaguered city.

Vaudreuil, who had been one of the first to leave Quebec for Montreal, wrote to the Minister of Marine in France blaming the whole débâcle on Ramezai, Montcalm, Bougainville and de Bourlamaque. On Ramezai he threw

the blame for the capitulation, but it was on Montcalm's conduct that he cast
the greatest aspersions, with a bitterness that the General's death heightened
rather than allayed.

> Far from seeking conciliation, he did nothing but try to persuade the
> public that his authority surpassed mine. From the moment of M. de
> Montcalm's arrival in this colony, down to the time of his death, he
> did not cease to sacrifice everything to his boundless ambition. He
> sowed dissension among the troops, tolerated the most indecent talk
> against the government, attached himself to the most indecent
> persons, used means to corrupt the most virtuous and when he could
> not succeed, became their cruel enemy. He wished to become Gover-
> nor-General. He privately flattered with favours and promises of
> patronage every officer of the colony troops who adopted his ideas. . . .
> He and Bougainville, his aide-de-camp, defamed honest people,
> encouraged insubordination and closed their eyes to the rapine of his
> soldiers.

At the same time, for some devious reason, he wrote to the Minister of War
how much he deplored the death of Montcalm, "this gallant and so brilliant
officer". Francis Parkman comments,

> His charges are strange ones from a man who was by turns the patron,
> advocate and tool of the official villains who cheated the King and
> plundered the people. Bigot, Cadet and the rest of the harpies that
> preyed on Canada looked to Vaudreuil for support and found it. It
> was but three or four weeks since the Governor had written to the
> Court in high eulogy of Bigot and effusive praise of Cadet, coupled
> with the request that a patent of nobility should be given to that
> notorious public thief. (*Montcalm and Wolfe*, vol. II.)

The corruptions which disgraced his government were rife not only in the civil
administration, but also among the officers of the colonial troops, over whom
he had complete control. The officers of the line, however, were above peculation. It was these who were the habitual associates of Montcalm and Bougainville, and whom Vaudreuil, because they were not of his own party, charged as
"disreputable".

He says, further, that Montcalm lost the battle at Quebec by attacking before
he (Vaudreuil) could take control. This, he says, was owing to Montcalm's
absolute determination to exercise independent authority, without caring
whether the colony was saved or lost, and so on and so on.

Ten days later Vaudreuil wrote again. "I have already had the honour, by
my letter in cipher of the 30th of last month [30 October 1759], to give you a

sketch of the character of M. Le Marquis de Montcalm; but I have just been informed of a stroke so black that I think, Monseigneur, that I should fail in my duty if I did tell you of it."

The stroke so black was that "fearful, no doubt, of the fate that befell him" Montcalm had placed in the hands of a Franciscan missionary two packets of papers criticizing the administration of the colony and especially the manner in which the military posts were furnished with supplies; that these observations were accompanied by certificates; and that they involved charges against Vaudreuil of complicity in peculation. The missionary was to send the papers to France; "but now, Monseigneur, that you are informed about them, I feel no anxiety, and I am sure that the King will receive no impression from them without acquainting himself with their truth or falsity".

Vaudreuil's anxiety was natural. It would seem that he was unaware that Bougainville had already complained of the widespread corruption in Canada, though he must have had some hint of this when he received orders to consult with Montcalm on all matters pertaining to the defence of the colony and to avoid all differences with him. Montcalm's action in making known to the Court the abuses that threatened the King's service was also quite natural, for the sake both of the public good and of the justification of his own conduct.

Later, when Vaudreuil and others were brought to trial in Paris, and when one of the counsel for the defence charged the dead general with having slanderously accused his clients, the Court ordered the charge to be deleted from the record. But I anticipate.

Each time, during the various campaigns, when it had become necessary to discuss terms of capitulation, it was invariably Bougainville who had been appointed the intermediary to negotiate the settlement between victor or vanquished. Once again, after the fall of Quebec, it was the young Colonel who was detailed to treat with the English General Townshend, who from the eighteenth of September, had occupied the town, the very day of its surrender. Townshend, it will be remembered, had been a close acquaintance of Bougainville while the latter had been in England, and, even throughout the war, had remained in friendly correspondence with the brilliant scholar–soldier; it was only natural, therefore, that he should give Bougainville a most courteous reception and do all in his power to facilitate his task. Arrangements were made for senior French officers to pass the winter months in Montreal on parole. Townshend arranged for medical care to be given to the French sick and wounded and provided what victuals he could for the starving population. Before embarking for England, where he had been ordered to give an account of Wolfe's glorious victory, Townshend wrote a personal letter to Bougainville bidding him farewell and concluding with words eloquent of the esteem and friendship he bore him: 'In spite of the many friends you have in England, I beg of you to allow me the honour of interesting myself on your behalf and on that of your acquaintances.'

The French General Staff had retired to Montreal for the winter, while Townshend had been succeeded by General Murray as commander of Quebec. Despite the loss of Quebec and lack of support from France, the Chevalier de Lévis refused to despair and was busy preparing plans for the next campaign. Bougainville, utterly exhausted, was ordered to take to his bed and husband his strength. Strangely enough this order came from Vaudreuil himself. It was an atrocious winter, worse than Bougainville had ever experienced. 'The time has come,' he wrote to his *chère maman*, 'I have spent close on eighty sleepless nights, suffered indescribable fatigues and gone through miseries of a kind unknown in Europe.' Once again, in addition to the cold, were added the burdens of famine. Costs of provisions soared to unbelievable prices. Had it not been for de Lévis's magnetic personality and fortitude, the morale of the army could not have survived that terrible winter. But somehow this extraordinary young commander in-chief, junior in rank to Vaudreuil, succeeded in sustaining the *esprit-de-corps* of his depleted army.

At the end of March 1760 Bougainville was chosen to command the Île-aux-Noix, a little island in the Richelieu river, eight leagues south of Montreal and two north of Lake Champlain. It forms a natural barrier in the course of the river from the lake to the St Lawrence, and so was of great strategic importance. The post of commander there had previously been filled by de Bourlamaque, but with the death of Montcalm he had become second-in-command of the army. Bougainville would much have preferred to stay at the side of de Lévis, but by the rules of seniority it was he who succeeded to the defence of the little island, and, good soldier that he was, he obeyed orders.

By the end of April de Lévis had so successfully reorganized his forces that on the 28th, near the village of St Foy, on the outer ring of Quebec's defences, he gained a brilliant victory and repeated, though with the roles reversed, the incidents of the battle on the Plains of Abraham. Murray's soldiers had been routed and had sought safety within the walls of Quebec. "*Ma foi*," Bougainville wrote to Lévis, "since you have retrieved our honour, you shall be our father; and even if you should not recapture the town, none the less you will be crowned with glory. Ah, *mon général*, you did not allow me to be at your side. I am wounded to the heart. But in this trade of ours one must obey and not choose. . . . Nothing new here, we work while you win battles."

Britain and her American colonies had decided to make one last mighty effort to strike a decisive blow at Canada. A fleet of frigates with strong reinforcements were sent across the ocean. Three British armies invaded New France—with Montreal, the only town there that remained to be conquered, as their objective. General Amherst, who was Commander-in-Chief, advanced by

Lake Ontario, and Brigadier Havilland by way of Lake Champlain. Murray, with the remains of his army defeated at St Foy, set out to join the others and so play his part. In Thiéry's words, "they encircled in a ring of iron the heroic fragments of the French army, which, deprived of all help and without hope, awaited the final struggle in Montreal".

On 9 August, Havilland's army came in sight of the Île-aux-Noix, which Bougainville had done his best to fortify. After sixteen days of intense bombardment, Bougainville, with only two days' provisions left, was forced to follow Vaudreuil's advice that he should evacuate the island before the last extremity was reached. At a council of war he and his officers unanimously agreed that the evacuation should be carried out immediately. There was no purpose in sacrificing further lives there; better far to join de Lévis at Montreal. Bougainville embarked his men that very same night in the greatest secrecy, without the knowledge of the British; but, owing to the ignorance of his guides, his little army went astray. After a march of one whole night and half the next day, they once more found themselves within half a league of Île-aux-Noix, only a short distance from the enemy outposts. It was then that one of the French soldiers had the happy idea of creeping up behind the British and stealing a superb horse for Bougainville, who was no longer strong enough to continue the journey on foot.

In the meanwhile de Lévis had sent a request to France that a ship laden with munitions and heavy siege-guns should be sent to meet him after the ice broke up at Quebec in April, when he could also expect the arrival of a ship that had wintered at Gaspé. The arrival of these vessels would have made the position of the British doubly critical; but, on the other hand, should a British squadron appear first, de Lévis would be forced to raise the siege. Both French and British watched the river with increasing anxiety, though not forgetting to maintain the courtesies usual in eighteenth-century warfare. De Lévis, who had heard that Murray liked spruce beer, sent Bougainville to him under a flag of truce with a quantity of spruce boughs and a message of compliment; Murray responded with a Cheshire cheese; and de Lévis then sent a present of partridges.

On 9 May a man o' war was observed bearing up towards the town. The news soon spread; men and officers, divided between hope and fear, crowded to the ramparts and every eye was strained on the approaching ship. Was she British or was she French? Slowly her colours rose to the masthead and were revealed as those of the Royal Navy; it was the British frigate *Lowestoffe* (*sic*). The British celebrated her arrival with shout on shout and discharges of salvos of artillery for almost an hour. She brought news that a British squadron was at the mouth of the St Lawrence and would reach Quebec within a few days.

De Lévis, ignorant of the approach of a British squadron, still clung to the hope that French vessels would arrive, with the supplies he had requested. A week later, however, on the evening of the 15th, a British ship of the line, HMS *Vanguard*, and the frigate *Diane* sailed into the harbour. The next morning they passed the town to attack the French vessels in the river above. These were six in all: two frigates, two sloops and two schooners, under the command of Admiral Vauquelin. In the ensuing engagement Vauquelin fought from his flagship—a mere frigate—with persistent bravery, and even when his ammunition was spent refused to strike his colours. He was eventually taken prisoner, and was treated by his captors with great honour. The other vessels put up little or no resistance.

The destruction of the French vessels was the death blow to the hopes of de Lévis. He had passed the preceding night in great agitation, and, when the cannonade on the river ceased, he hastened to raise the siege, realizing that there was now no hope of capturing the city. He therefore ordered his army to fall back at night in the greatest secrecy, but deserters from the French informed Murray that the enemy was in full flight. Murray opened fire through the darkness, sending cannonballs *en ricochet*, bowling by scores together over the Plains of Abraham at the heels of the retiring enemy. At dawn the following day, the British marched out in pursuit, but the French, leaving a vast amount of equipment behind, had already crossed the river at Cap Rouge and were heading for Montreal.

Alas, de Lévis's victory at St Foy had proved to be nothing more than a brilliant episode—one last gleam of glory in the course of a hopeless struggle.

The retreat of de Lévis left Canada little hope but in a speedy peace. Murray so successfully revitalized his sick and wounded garrison that he was able to put about 2,500 men into the field to support General Amherst in a final attack to reduce Montreal. Amherst, it will be recollected, had resolved to enter the colony by way of three gates at once: Brigadier Havilland by way of Lake Champlain; Murray by the St Lawrence, from Quebec; and himself, leading the main army, down the St Lawrence from Lake Ontario. Despite a brave resistance by the French, the British forces were united beneath the walls of Montreal on 6 September.

On the night of the same day, Vaudreuil called together at the Château a council of war of his principal officers, including Bougainville. All were of the same mind: they declared that, in view of the state of the army, by then reduced to an effective strength of only 2,132 soldiers, lacking in almost every means of defence, "resistance should not be pushed to the last extremity, and that it was better to arrange a capitulation that would be advantageous to the people and honourable to the troops, who would thus be saved for the King, than maintain a stubborn defence that could only pospone by a few days the loss of the country". The Governor then had a plan of surrender read out, and all agreed to it.

On the morning of 7 September, Bougainville, as usual chosen as the one to negotiate terms, set out, accompanied by a captain, four cavalrymen and a drummer, in the direction of the British outposts that lay beneath the walls of the town. He carried to General Amherst the offer of the surrender of the colony. The General, who had neither the nobility of character of Wolfe nor the courtesy of Townshend, refused the honours of war to the heroic French armies and insisted that they should never again serve against the British.

The French officers to a man indignantly protested against such an humiliating clause. The Chevalier de Lévis, supported by Bougainville, declared that he would prefer a last decisive combat to complete inaction while war continued to drag out its course in Germany. On the following day, Bougainville returned once more to protest against Amherst's stipulation. The General, however, was unyielding, and the French could do nothing but submit. De Lévis broke his sword in two and ordered his officers "to burn their colours and so escape the harsh condition which demanded their surrender to the enemy".

On 8 September the capitulation of Montreal was signed. To quote Maurice Thiéry,

> In spite of long years of bloody struggles, in spite of the nobility of an entire people, and the heroism of its armies, in spite of the genius of immortal leaders, the most splendid of all French colonies, abandoned by the distant motherland, fell to the hands of England. So ended the war in Canada.

The artist's painting of the Port of Brest at it was when Bougainville had his ship refitted, after a contemporary engraving.

BOOK TWO

ROUND THE WORLD

The Drymis, found by Winter but discovered by
Commerson and named "Magelliana".

Commerson called this "Dorwallia" but it was later renamed *Fuchsia Magellanica* by Lamark.

Chapter One

The Peace of Paris, 1762–3

In accordance with the terms of the capitulation of Montreal, all the French military officers and those of the French regular soldiers who could be kept together, plus all senior French civil officials, sailed for France in ships provided by the British. They were voluntarily followed by a number of the Canadian *noblesse*, and by merchants who had no wish to serve under the flag of King George. The departure of the leaders of Canada was, however, deferred until the year after the capitulation, for it was difficult for the British to find sufficient vessels to convey such a motley crowd across the ocean, despite the defection of many French soldiers who had married Canadian wives. When, finally, the first convoy set sail, it was subjected to a series of terrifying autumnal storms, in which some ships were wrecked or driven ashore. The surviving vessels landed their passengers on the shores of France at the end of November. Some of the arrivals received, to their surprise and dismay, a far from pleasant welcome, being immediately placed under arrest and thrown into the Bastille. These included an indignant Vaudreuil, plus Bigot, Cadet and others of the ex-Governor's cronies whom Montcalm and Bougainville had accused of fraud and peculation. In December 1761 they were brought to trial. A prodigious amount of evidence was produced against them. Cadet, with brazen effrontery, at first declared himself innocent, but ended by making a full confession. Bigot denied everything until silenced with the production of papers bearing his own signature. The prisoners defended themselves by accusing each other. Bigot and Vaudreuil brought mutual charges, while all agreed in denouncing Cadet. Vaudreuil was acquitted. Bigot was banished from France for life, his property was confiscated, and he was ordered by the Court to pay 1,500,000 livres in compensation; Cadet was banished from Paris for nine years and ordered to refund 6 millions; the sentences of the other guilty men were commensurate.

For his part, Bougainville was hailed as a hero at the Court of Versailles, where Madame de Pompadour and her great friend Choiseul (now the most powerful and far-sighted minister in France) received him with every demonstration of affection. He was esteemed as a man of action and rated high above the crowd of useless courtiers. But idle life at Court irked him; his restless spirit demanded action. He offered Versailles his services, which were immediately

accepted. In 1761 he was appointed to accompany the Duc de Praslin to Augs-
burg, with the object of attending a conference to discuss the possibilities of
peace. To his great disappointment the conference did not take place; he therefore took the necessary steps to obtain from the British Court release from his
parole, but it was not until the following year that he finally received permission
to serve again and that in Europe only.

In May 1762, the Duc de Choiseul, as Secretary of State for War and for the
Navy, despatched Bougainville as the bearer of special instructions to Marshals
d'Estrées and Soubise, who were commanding part of the armies in Germany.
On 11 July, he was appointed to the staff of the Comte de Stainville, who with
several regiments was marching on Hirschfeld in order to re-establish touch
with the Prince de Condé. Although there was some skirmishing, during
which Bougainville was slightly wounded, the Anglo-Prussian forces, to his
chagrin, refused confrontation. Impatient at this inactivity, Bougainville was
allowed to return to Versailles and report to the King on the state of affairs in
the theatre of war. As a reward for his services to the army in Germany, he was
presented with two pieces of cannon—a cumbersome but honorific gift—
which were installed on his estate at La Brosse, between Brie and Melun.

For France one disaster followed another. Britain was paramount at sea and
on land. The white banner of France emblazoned with the fleur-de-lys no
longer floated over the ports of India or on the plains of Canada; the sugar-
producing colonies of Martinique and La Guadeloupe and other islands of the
Americas had fallen to British arms; and even Belle Isle, off the coast of Brittany,
saw the redcoats in possession of its outer ring of forts.

It was about this time that Bougainville petitioned Choiseul to seek permission from the British for him to serve at sea. The Duke of Bedford, who was
then (1762) representing the British in Paris with a view to negotiating a peace,
immediately gave his consent. Complete liberty of action, without reservation
of any kind, was accorded to the young and impatient colonel. Mme Hérault,
on learning the news, was in tears. She had lost her own son at Minden, and
Louis-Antoine, who had miraculously survived the war in America and a
dangerous mission to Germany, was now voluntarily exposing himself to further
dangers.

Bougainville received immediate orders to proceed to Dunkirk to take
command of a corps of 2,000 men, who were then to join up with a similar
force, destined to sail from Brest under the command of the Comte d'Estaing,
to recapture the lost islands of the Antilles. But, just as Bougainville was about
to leave to take up his appointment, he learned, to his disgust, that a separate
peace had been negotiated between Britain and France at Fontainebleau on 3
November 1762, eventually to be ratified in February of the following year.
Bougainville gave vent to an explosion of impotent rage on learning of this
disastrous treaty, by which France regained Martinique, La Guadeloupe and
Belle Isle, but officially ceded to Britain nearly all her possessions in India and

eastern North America. Moreover, by a secret agreement made in Madrid, she ceded Louisiana to Spain, so divesting herself of her last territorial possession on the North American continent.

Bougainville realized that the treaty concluded at Fontainebleau constituted the foundation of British world power; but what could he, a colonel of thirty-four years of age, do to rectify such a disaster? Feeling that he must make at least some attempt to restore France's colonial and maritime fortunes, he set his mind to the task. He recalled that only the previous year Admiral Lord Anson, just before his death, had reminded the British Government that the Royal Navy, being unsurpassed in power by any other navy, should immediately be employed to extend Britain's maritime possessions by occupying the many as yet uncharted, but reputedly fabulously rich, islands of the Pacific Ocean. He had proposed that permission should be sought from Portugal to refit a small flotilla in Rio de Janeiro, and that this flotilla should thence sail to the uninhabited Falkland Islands, to which, as yet, no country laid claim. (Known in France as the Malouines, or Isles of St Malo, they were, however, frequented by French whalers.) These would be strategically invaluable as a point of departure for voyages to the Pacific Ocean via the Straits of Magellan.

Bougainville knew too much about the practical and acquisitive spirit of the British to imagine that there would be any delay in acting on the advice of their great admiral. "What interest should the English have in doing otherwise," he wrote in his Journal, "than secure in the interval of a peace such as the present a base which at the first sign of another war would place them in the position of the arbiters of Europe?" If France were to forestall the British in their designs, she must act immediately. Bougainville put his plans before his King, who, on the advice of Choiseul, gave them his immediate approval and appointed the young colonel to the rank of brevet-captain of the navy. At the same time, however, he was obliged to point out that, although the scheme met with his entire approval and that of his ministers, the public exchequer was, as usual, empty. Not to be outdone, Bougainville, ever a man of resource, assured His Most Christian Majesty that he was prepared to take upon himself the responsibility for financing the expedition. He floated a company—the Compagnie de St Malo—to which many of his wealthy shipowner friends subscribed. His ever-generous uncle d'Arboulin gladly opened his purse to him once his nephew had explained his plans. It was the same with his generous cousin M. de Nerville, who placed all his vast credit at his relative's disposal. Well provided with all these precious offerings, to which he added almost all his own personal fortune, he set out for St Malo. Bougainville loved the hardy Bretons of St Malo, who had provided France with so many great mariners and so many proud vessels, and who now so generously invested in Bougainville's new company. He sought out a M. Duclos-Guyot, who had previously accompanied him on his journeys to and from Canada. Duclos-Guyot not only fell in with Bougainville's new plans but also offered to build an armed frigate of twenty guns, to be named the

Aigle, and a sloop of twelve guns, the *Sphinx*, to Bougainville's own specific-
ations. He even offered to act as second-in-command of the frigate, the crew of
which was to consist of one hundred men, including his brother Alexandre, who
was familiar with the Southern Ocean and the Straits of Magellan. Bougainville
accepted his offer with enthusiasm. The sloop, manned by a crew of forty, was
to be commanded by a M. Chénard de la Giraudais. The vessels were christened
in August at St Servant, near St Malo, with the usual ceremony. While mass
was being sung, two salvos of cannon were fired—one for God and one for the
King. At the beginning of September men and provisions were taken aboard.
The project conceived only a few months previously had now become a reality.

On 15 September 1763, Bougainville, eager for the unknown, sailed with
his two vessels out of St Malo. The officer of the royal armies faded into the
past; the sailor had been born.

Chapter Two

The Falkland Islands, 1763–4

Bougainville was accompanied by a very distinguished staff, including Étienne de Belcourt, captain of infantry; Denys de St Simon, an officer of Canadian origin; and a Monsieur de L'Huillier, an army geographer and engineer. He was also accompanied by his cousin de Nerville, who had helped to finance the expedition, and Dom Antoine-Joseph Pernetty of the Benedictine community of St Maur, who was to perform the offices of chaplain. The activities of this erudite priest were by no means confined to theology; he was also an eminent naturalist, botanist, Egyptologist, and no mean artist. Alexander Dumas *père* tells an amusing if apocryphal story of how Bougainville lured this priest on board his ship against the latter's will and detained him over dinner until the vessel was well out to sea, too late for the good man to return to his parish.

Since one must have colonists in order to found a colony, Bougainville had taken some twenty men (bachelors) and three families of Acadians (Nova Scotians), thirty-six in all, with him. It will be recollected that, ever since the Treaty of Utrecht, Nova Scotia had been a British colony. The simple inhabitants had enjoyed a peaceful and calm life under a humane British rule, free to practise their own religion and choose their own priests. Many had been born under the British flag, and, had it not been for the machinations of a bigoted and malicious priest, Father Le Loutre from Quebec, Vicar-General of Nova Scotia, the Acadians might have continued to live a contented life. But the simple Acadians, mostly of Breton stock, were a superstitious and deeply religious people. Le Loutre lost no opportunity in stressing to them that, should they ever take an oath of allegiance to heretics, they were for ever damned. He even stirred up Indian tribes to attack farmsteads whose owners preferred to stay in Nova Scotia and take an oath of allegiance to Britain than to return to French Canada. A combination of the fiery oratory of Le Loutre and his self-appointed priests and the fear engendered by Indian raids drove many of the inhabitants to leave for Canada or take up arms against the British garrisons and settlers. Naturally the British were forced to retaliate against these dissident misled colonists—hence Monkton's attack on Fort Beauséjour (see above, Book I, ch. 2). The unfortunate Acadians who were persuaded by their priests to leave for Canada now found themselves treated as unwelcome beggars. When Bougainville arrived in Quebec he was appalled at the starving condition of these once-industrious farmers and fishermen, who were completely neglected by Canadian government agents. Many Acadians preferred to escape to the British colonies. Strangely enough, it was the Quaker colonists of Pennsylvania and the Lutheran Germans of the Palatine flats who gave the warmest welcome to these unfortunate Catholics. Some Acadians preferred to go to Britain; others asked to be returned to Brittany, where the parismonious government of Louis XV provided them with such meagre assistance that most were reduced to abject poverty. The lot of these unfortunate families had never been far from the thoughts of the generous-hearted Bougainville.

The fortunate few given the opportunity to travel to the Falkland Islands, where they anticipated manifold advantages which they could not hope for in France, eagerly accepted the proposal, all the more so since Bougainville, in the name of the King, had already made them advances of money and goods. Only one family proved ungrateful and unco-operative. "Since poverty suits you," said Bougainville, "go and live in poverty", and promptly put them ashore at St Cast, near St Malo. Ever generous, however, he allowed them to retain the money and goods already advanced to them.

On 29 November the ships crossed the Equator. This the passengers and crew marked by the quaint and bizarre ceremony of "Crossing the Line", which Dom Pernetty, in his Journal, describes in detail, and in which Bougainville and his officers goodnaturedly participated. Although such ceremonies were much more crude and uninhibited in those days than they would be in the years to come, Bougainville's participation much increased his popularity with crew and passengers.

On 14 January 1764 the *Aigle* put in at the Portuguese island of St Catherine, off the coast of Brazil. Bougainville prepared to take in provisions of wood and supplies of fresh drinking water. The Portuguese Governor warmly welcomed Bougainville and his staff and entertained them to a friendly, but, to sophisticated French palates, indifferent, meal, relieved only by the Governor's excellent Port wine. Present at the dinner was a Franciscan monk, whom Dom Pernetty addressed in Latin, the international language among all clerics of the day. The embarrassed monk, who understood not a single word of his colleague's Latin eloquence, slipped quietly away at the close of the dinner to escape the literary conversation of the learned Benedictine. On the following day, Bougainville returned the Governor's hospitality aboard the *Aigle*. An awning was erected on the quarter-deck and the ship was dressed with bunting from stem to stern; Dom Pernetty celebrated mass and then the subjects of the King of Portugal sat down to a sumptuous meal to enjoy the delights of French cooking and some of France's most excellent wines, to the accompaniment of hautboys, violins and timpani.

The *Aigle* remained at St Catherine for two weeks. Bougainville, accompanied by the naturalist Pernetty and other members of his staff, made expeditions into the interior of the island and to the mainland. The densely forested country proved a perpetual joy to Pernetty, who observed with delight the multicoloured parakeets and other wonderful birds, but whose enthusiasm was not altogether shared by other members of the party. The roar of the jaguar, the realization that the forest was infested with poisonous snakes, and the sight of hordes of huge monkeys disporting themselves, as Pernetty reports, "in a thousand strange antics" all served to discourage them. Pernetty also took every opportunity to study the natives of the island and their customs. He found them a kindly, hospitable people, devoted and loyal to their friends, but with "a taste for the flesh of their enemies".

After an exchange of presents—the French giving the Portuguese exquisite fans and snuff-boxes, and the Portuguese presenting the French with domestic animals, birds and a tame jaguar, on 14 December the *Aigle* set off again and made sail for the Spanish port of Montevideo. In the course of the journey the crew were, with regret, obliged to kill the jaguar, whose voracious appetite was too quickly diminishing their rations, and whose roars continually interrupted their sleep.

The *Aigle* cast anchor at Montevideo on 26 December and were welcomed at first coldly, though politely, by the Governor. He made it abundantly clear that he was not prepared to render all the services Bougainville required of him, including the provision of cattle on the hoof, horses and wood. "Monsieur," said Bougainville, "it is indeed hard that Frenchmen should meet from their friends the Spanish with difficulties which they did not encounter from the Portuguese, with whom, not so short a time ago, they were at war. I shall put to sea at once, but I shall give an account of this to the King my master." These initial differences were soon resolved, however, and an exchange of courtesies took place. The dinner that the Governor gave for Bougainville and his officers was, though, described by Bougainville in his Journal as "atrocious and the wine pharmaceutical".

During three months in Montevideo the French had ample opportunity to study Spanish colonial habits, chief of which appeared to be idleness. When not enjoying a siesta, the men sat enjoying a cigar and listening to their womenfolk strumming the guitar. Dom Pernetty watched closely a dance known as the *calenda*, introduced by slaves from the Guinea Coast, and with righteous Benedictine indignation condemns it in his Journal as of a "voluptuous and lascivious character". In fact, on the whole, the moral code in this distant Spanish colony was what would now be called "permissive".

On 31 December, the *Sphinx*, which for the past two months had been out of touch with her sister ship, rejoined the *Aigle* in the bay of Montevideo; and two weeks later the ships set out for the Falkland Islands.

The Falkland Islands had been discovered in 1592 by the English navigator Davis. Drake had sighted them and Richard Hawkins, who had skirted their

northern shores, had first called them Virginia. In 1690, another Englishman,
Strong, gave them the name of his patron, Lord Falkland, while at the beginning
of the eighteenth century some Breton whalers from Saint Malo gave them the
adjectival name of "Malouines", after their native port. But little was known
about the islands until 1764, when Bougainville landed there. The *Aigle* and the
Sphinx anchored in a wonderful bay. At seven o'clock on the evening of 2
February 1764, Donat de Lagarde, First Lieutenant of the *Sphinx*, became the
first man to be put ashore there. His report proving favourable, crew and
passengers disembarked the following day. Bougainville and Pernetty's first
impressions were hardly encouraging. Bougainville described what he saw as

> A landscape bounded on the horizon by bleak mountains; the fore-
> ground eroded by the sea, which seems to be ever struggling for
> supremacy; a countryside lifeless for lack of inhabitants; neither
> pasture lands nor forest for the encouragement of those who were
> destined to become the first colonists; a vast silence, broken only by
> the cry of a sea monster; everywhere a sad and melancholy uniformity.

His description borders on the romantic. De Lagarde, however, on first stepping
ashore, had been greeted by hundreds of friendly penguins, whom he describes
looking like so many choirboys in black and white cottas.

It was only natural that, in these first hours of contact with this distant land,
crew and passengers should suffer from pangs of homesickness; but it was thanks
largely to Dom Pernetty that the would-be settlers became reassured. This
industrious priest, accompanied by members of the crew, ventured, armed with
musket and bayonet and with the skirts of his habit gathered up, into the interior. He discovered that first appearances had been deceptive. There were
rivers and waterfalls; plains covered with rich pasture and ideal for grazing;
lakes and pools abounding in fish; game birds in plenty—duck of all kinds,
delicate and appetizing bustards, snipe and wild geese and grouse—so tame that
they could be caught by hand. There were also edible plants that proved to be
excellent against scurvy. Sealions and seals abounded to provide oil. All that
was missing to make a perfect colony was timber, for the islands were altogether
treeless. In their ignorance, the sailors shot a quite unnecessary number of seals
and sealions and burnt down a great deal of the highly combustible heather and
rough grassland, destroying many of the game birds in the process.

By 17 March Bougainville had decided where to found the capital of his
colony. The site lay about three miles from the head of the bay, beside a small
natural harbour connected to the open waters by a narrow channel. Without
delay, sailors set about building huts and storehouses with the timber provided
by the Governor of Montevideo, while Bougainville and other members of the
crew, including M. de L'Huillier, his engineer, began building a fortress of
earth and turf sods, with emplacements for fourteen cannon. They toiled for a

fortnight from dawn to dusk, till eventually the fort was finished. It was then solemnly named Fort St Louis. In the centre of the little citadel, a pillar twenty feet high was raised, and on the top of it was placed a bust of Louis XV modelled in clay by Pernetty. But the clay proved too soft and the bust disintegrated, leaving only the head. The carpenter of the *Sphinx* saved the situation by carving a fleur-de-lis on a piece of wood and the inscription "Tibi serviat Ultima Thule" ("Ultima Thule serves you"). On the opposite side of the pillar, on another piece of wood, was engraved the act of possession of the Malouines.

The formal act of occupation followed. Coins and medals were engraved with, on the obverse, the date of the enterprise (February 1764) and the names of the principal members of the expedition, and, on the reverse, the words "Conumar tenues grandia" ("Small though we are we attempt a mighty task"). A number of these coins and medals were buried at the base of the pillar.

Then, in the presence of all, the monument was unveiled. A shout of "Vive le Roy" was repeated seven times, followed by a salute of twenty-one guns. Finally Bougainville displayed the King's patent appointing the Governor of the new colony and presented it to de Nerville, who was immediately received and acknowledged as such. On 5 April Bougainville took formal possession of the Falkland Islands in the name of the King, and on the 8th he set out again for France, aboard the *Aigle*, to a further salute of guns. On 26 June a happy and proud Bougainville disembarked at St Malo.

He immediately set out for Versailles to give an account of his voyage to his King, who confirmed his annexation of the Malouines. Choiseul, the Minister of Marine, gave orders "to support the settlement and increase it". The *Aigle* was refitted, and on 6 October in the same year the frigate, again commanded by Bougainville, and with a crew of 116 and fifty-three new colonists, once more set sail for the south.

On 5 January 1765 the *Aigle* put in at the harbour near the fortress of St Louis. Bougainville and his crew and passengers were welcomed with enthusiasm. The healthy and happy appearance of the first settlers was clear evidence of the success of their new colonial life in this distant outpost in the ocean. The cattle and horses brought there on the first voyage were in perfect condition. The plants and vegetables introduced from Europe had flourished beyond all expectations. De Nerville, who seemed in no way to regret the contrast between his present way of life and the *vie mondaine* of Paris, had constructed new store-houses and a powder magazine and had strengthened the fortress. Bougainville was radiant with joy. The only serious difficulty was the complete lack of timber, and to make good this deficiency he almost immediately decided to explore the shores of the Straits of Magellan. Alexandre Duclos-Guyot, who had already had experience of these dreaded waters, acted as navigator.

On entering the straits they were surprised to sight three ships flying the British flag, and, a few days later, when one of these was seen to founder on the rocky shore, Bougainville made haste to send two lifeboats to its aid. The little

British squadron was commanded by Commodore Byron, uncle of the poet. He too had recently come from the Falkland Islands, where he had anchored west of the French settlement, in a natural harbour that Bougainville had named Port Crusade, but that Byron had called Port Egmont. The British Commodore had not hesitated, on landing, to claim possession of the islands for the British Crown, a claim regarded by Bougainville as untenable, since no representative or settlers had been left there. It was not until the following year (1766) that the British sent out some settlers, mostly of Scottish stock. The captain who brought them, Bougainville afterwards recorded, "claimed that these territories belonged to the British Crown. He threatened to force a landing if any obstacle were put in his way, but then, after paying a brief visit to the Governor, sailed away the same day."

Although the sea was calm and the weather fine, Bougainville proceeded through the Straits of Magellan with caution. At last he came to a little bay surrounded by dense forest. This bay, where Bougainville ordered that they should anchor, the sailors named after their leader.

For three weeks, one and all, Bougainville and his officers included, worked at hewing down trees, hauling logs to the beach, squaring timbers into huge blocks, hoisting them on board, and then stacking them for shipment. "We also carefully lifted and carried on board", writes Bougainville, "more than 10,000 seedlings from trees of different ages, and the establishment of plantations on our islands was a most interesting experiment."

During the course of these laborious tasks, some native Patagonians nervously approached the French. For years it had been believed that Patagonian natives were fearsome creatures at least seven to eight feet tall (even Commodore Byron, in his report, says this) covered with fur and possessing tails; so it was with surprise that the French found the natives to be gentle creatures of normal height, with a strong dislike for alcohol but a predilection for fatty foods. Bougainville gave them a quantity of red flannel, a French flag and cooking utensils, and made them cry "Vive le Roy". Bougainville thought it well worthwhile to gain the friendship of these nearest neighbours of the new French colony. On 29 March, he returned to Fort St Louis, "having", as he himself expressed it, "opened up a seaway as necessary for the support of the colony".

Happy with the progress and expansion of the new settlement, he returned to France on 27 April. Little did he know that all his enterprise and hard work in establishing the colony would soon be nullified, by the cession of these hard-won islands to Spain.

At Versailles, Bougainville gave an enthusiastic account of the colony's growing prosperity and had no difficulty in obtaining the King's authority to despatch to the islands, towards the end of 1765, the now overhauled and re-fitted *Aigle*, accompanied by the supply ship *Étoile*. Bougainville did not on this occasion take part in the expedition, Duclos-Guyot being in command of the frigate and de la Giraudais having charge of the second vessel. After landing a number of new colonists, as well as provisions and equipment, the two ships set sail for the Straits of Magellan, to obtain a further supply of wood.

On the shores of the straits a score or so of savages attacked some sailors from the *Aigle* who had spent the night on land. Having no opportunity to use their firearms, they had to defend themselves as best they could with axes and cutlasses. Three of the natives were killed and two of the French wounded.

The *Étoile*, on the other hand, had more friendly dealings with the Patagonians, with whom Bougainville had been so anxious for the French to be on good terms. De la Giraudais and Denys de St Simon did their very best to ensure this. Presents of meat, pipes and tobacco were exchanged, and the savages displayed their graceful wives, who, like women of the present day, were in the habit of plucking their eyebrows. Jealousy seemed to be something unknown among the people of those regions, for they encouraged the by no means unwilling French sailors to caress, in the most intimate manner, their wives and daughters. Henceforward, friendship prevailed.

The vessels returned to the Falkland Islands, where the colony continued to develop steadily. Three ammunition stores had been built, as well as two more schooners. A cargo of oil and dressed sealskins was despatched to France. Most of the seed brought from Europe had rapidly become acclimatized in this relatively temperate region; the livestock was increasing; and by the year 1766 the population had increased to 150 souls. Bougainville had every reason to congratulate himself on his initiative in founding the colony, which showed every sign of having a prosperous future in store.

In the meantime Britain had officially laid claim to the Falklands, and Choiseul, anxious at all costs to avoid a renewal of hostilities between France and Britain, might well have yielded to Britain's claim, had it not been that Spain—on learning that the British claim rested on the slender excuse of Commodore Byron's short visit to Fort Egmont, and that Captain Wallis, commanding the *Dolphin* (Byron's former ship) and accompanied by the *Swallow* (captained by Philip Carteret) and the *Prince Frederick*, was preparing to put to sea from Plymouth on 22 August 1766—immediately reacted by placing a counter-claim.

Bougainville, though in almost every respect a most brilliant man and respected leader, had allowed his enthusiasm as a colonist to cloud his political vision. It should have been clearly apparent to him from his cool reception by the Governor of Montevideo that Spain was far from anxious that either the British or the French should occupy the Falklands and that she was only awaiting the opportunity to claim them for herself as an integral part of her South American possessions.

Choiseul, who was forever changing his mind, now decided that, from France's viewpoint, it was better that Bourbon Spain should occupy the Malouines than that Britain should do so; indeed, ever since 1764, before Bougainville's second journey to the islands, he and the Duc de Praslin (the Minister of Marine) had been considering the possibility of acquiring the Philippines (in which the Spaniards were showing scant interest) in exchange. Since 1765 he had been negotiating with Madrid. Sad as he was at the thought of losing what he had begun to think of as his own colony, Bougainville was one of the first to see the advantages of such an exchange. British trade with China was still negligible and much of the Pacific Ocean remained uncharted, with America no more than a name. So far only Magellan, Drake, Roggeveen and Anson had circum-navigated the world, and the potential of the Pacific Ocean was practically unknown.

Again speed was essential, lest the British should take possession. Final negotiations with Spain had to be conducted, and the settlers, who preferred to leave their island homes, were to be evacuated. In the meantime, vessels to accommodate them were commissioned and refitted for the journey. It is highly probable that, even before Louis XV had been consulted, Praslin had ordered work to be put in hand, for in the incredibly short space of three months a new frigate, the *Boudeuse*, of twenty-five guns, was built at Nantes, and the *Aigle* and the *Étoile* were entirely overhauled.

Naturally it was Bougainville who was ordered to Madrid to negotiate the final handover. Twice he rode on horseback from Versailles to Spain (for he was as skilful a rider as he was soldier, sailor and mathematician), making the journey there and back in record time. The negotiations did not take long. His main objective was to extract from the Spanish as much compensation as he could, both for himself and the settlers and for the French Government. The amount of the indemnity was agreed upon at 603,000 livres, to be paid partly in Paris and partly in Buenos Aires, and it was agreed that a new expedition should be despatched to the Falklands to arrange for the official transfer of the islands to the Spanish Government. There was no mention of the Philippines.

There was, of course, only one man capable of taking command of so deli-cate a mission—Bougainville. Without hesitation the Duc de Praslin (Madame de Pompadour had died in 1764) proposed his name to the King, who confirmed the Minister's choice and at the same time granted Bougainville the further authority he desired to prolong his voyage as far as the East Indies. Furthermore, in an unexpected act of generosity, he agreed to pay from the privy purse for all construction work on the *Boudeuse*, which was to be Bougainville's flagship.

Thus, after a short and flourishing existence of three years under the French flag, the Falklands were to pass into other hands.

Chapter Three

The Start of the Great Journey, 1766

For some time now, Bougainville had been irresistibly drawn to the sea, which alone could slake his burning thirst for the unknown. For him the sea held no fears; the boundless poetry of the ocean had gripped him, and he was fascinated by thought not only of voyaging to the East Indies, but of completing a circumnavigation of the globe.

Bougainville was ordered to join the completed *Boudeuse* at Nantes early in November 1766. There he met his friend Duclos-Guyot, who, with his brother Alexandre, was in charge of victualling and providing munitions for the new ship. He now assembled the brilliant staff that he had been at pains to select. These included the Chevalier de la Motte de Bourmand, the Chevalier d'Oraison, the Chevalier de Bouchage, the Chevaliers de Suzannet and Kervé (both midshipmen with the acting rank of officers), a surgeon named Laporte, and, as chaplain, Father Lavaisse, a Franciscan. Also on Bougainville's staff were three volunteers: one of the writers to the King, M. St-Germain, who was to be responsible for recording what happened during the voyage; Charles Félix Fesche, formerly a member of the crew of the *Aigle*; and, lastly, the twenty-one-year-old Prince Charles de Nassau-Siegen, a German prince but a French subject, "military by tradition and dilettante by vocation". He had been a captain of dragoons and was exceptionally handsome and daring. Charles-Nicolas-Othon de Nassau was, of all the passengers aboard the *Boudeuse*, one of the most extraordinary. After Bougainville's successful journey round the world, he served with the Spanish army and was in command of the artillery at the siege of Gibraltar. Later, after marrying a Polish princess, he sold his sword to Stanislas Augustus, King of Poland; next we find him a favourite of Catherine II of Russia and, with the rank of admiral, in command of the Russian naval forces in the Black Sea, fighting the Turks, and then in the Baltic, fighting the Swedes. He finally went into voluntary exile in the Ukraine. He made a short visit to France to propose to Napoleon a plan for the invasion of England, but on the rejection of this he returned to the Ukraine, where he died in 1808, at the age of sixty-five. He not only combined good looks with gracious manners, but, in addition, attracted Bougainville by the genuine interest he showed in maritime commerce and colonization. The *Boudeuse* was now all set and ready for sail.

Her sister ship, the *Étoile*, commissioned to carry the supplies, was under the command of de la Giraudais and was to sail from Rochefort and join the *Boudeuse* at the Falkland Islands. Bougainville's orders were to sail for the mouth of the river Plate in South America, where he was to meet the Spanish frigates *Esmeralda* and *Liebre*, whose commandant had been instructed to take over the Falkland Islands in the name of the King of Spain. Bougainville was to accompany the two Spanish vessels and officially transfer the colony, after which he would be free to pursue his journey of exploration into the mysteries of the Pacific.

The *Boudeuse* proceeded down the estuary of the Loire on 15 November. Two days later, however, a violent storm blew up, causing such serious damage to the masts that Bougainville found it essential to put into Brest for repairs; it was not until three weeks later, when shorter masts, designed to his own specification, were stepped, that the ship, with her full compliment of eleven officers, four volunteers, and a crew of one hundred men, including officers of the Marines, sailors, cabin boys and servants, was able to proceed on her voyage.

After an uneventful journey, on 31 January 1767 the *Boudeuse* cast anchor in the bay of Montevideo, on the left bank of the estuary of the river Plate, a short way below Buenos Aires. Two frigates floated at anchor in the bay. These were the two Spanish vessels charged with the duty of taking over the Falklands, of which their commandant, Don Luiz Puente, had been appointed Governor. After a friendly exchange of courtesies, Bougainville and Don Luiz decided to cross the estuary to Buenos Aires, to finalize with Don Francisco Bucarelli, Governor-General of the province of La Plata, who resided there, arrangements for the handover of the islands. Bougainville, accompanied by the Prince of Nassau-Siegen, made his way across the river in a schooner and landed on the outskirts of Buenos Aires. Don Francisco extended a most courteous welcome to the French commander. Official negotiations were soon completed and all the delicate financial points in connexion with the transfer were settled without difficulty or ill feeling.

His mission completed, Bougainville, with his insatiable desire for knowledge, was determined to explore the country and study the natives of the Argentine. He has left us in his Journal a most detailed account of his travels on horseback through these almost unknown territories, where he saw vast numbers of cattle and wild horses and was able to observe in detail the nature and life-style of the nomadic Indians who inhabited the area.

> Of the Indians inhabiting that part of America [he writes], those to the north and south of the river Plate are among those who have not yet been brought under the yoke of the Spaniards and who are called *Indios bravos*. They are of medium height, horribly ugly and nearly all

Michael Ross
del: The original
painting belongs to Mme la Baronne
de Vazeilhes.

Pen and ink portrait of Bougainville by the author.

show signs of skin disease. They have very swarthy complexions and the grease with which they are continually rubbing themselves makes them blacker still. Their only clothing consists of a great cloak of goatskin reaching to the knees. . . . Their principal weapon is the bow and arrow, but they also use the lasso and the "catapult" [i.e. the bolas]. The latter consists of two round, smooth stones—each about the size of a two-pound cannonball—attached separately to a strip of plaited cat-gut some six or seven feet long. They use this weapon from the saddle like a sling, and often bring down their quarry from a distance of as much as 200 yards. These Indians spend most of their lives on horseback and have no settled homes, at any rate not in the neighbourhood of the Spanish settlements. Sometimes, with their wives, they visit the towns to buy brandy and continue drinking until they have entirely lost the use of their limbs. To obtain strong liquor they will sell arms, skins and horses; and then, when all their means are exhausted, they will seize the first animals they can find and make off with them. Now and again, they collect in bands of two or three hundred and raid the cattle on properties belonging to the Spaniards or attack caravans of travellers. They pillage and massacre and carry off their surviving victims into slavery. It is an ill without remedy, for how is it possible to tame a race of nomads in a country so wild, so vast, that it would even be difficult to catch them? Besides, these Indians are brave and of warlike habit, and the times are past when one Spaniard could put to flight a thousand natives.

On account of unfavourable winds, Bougainville could not return to Montevideo in the schooner by which he had come, but had to make the journey by horse and canoe. He reached Montevideo again two weeks after he had left there.

On 28 February, after revictualling, the *Boudeuse* left in the company of the two Spanish frigates and set course for the Falkland Islands. There had been some difficulty in rounding up enough sailors, and would certainly have been greater trouble had it been known in advance that, almost immediately on leaving the estuary of the Plate, the ships would run into terrific storms, during which all the cattle that had been taken on board for the islanders perished. But on 25 March they made a safe landing at Fort St Louis, where Bougainville was given a rapturous welcome by the colonists. Their enthusiasm, however, quickly turned to dismay when they learned that the islands had officially been ceded to Spain. Those who wished to remain were permitted to do so, but the majority, including the whole of the administrative staff, opted to return with the Spanish frigates to Montevideo and thence to sail back to Europe or go wherever else they wished.

On 1 April the ceremony of handing over the islands was completed. The

D

white banner of France was lowered and the Spanish standard hoisted in its place. As Fesche, the official chronicler, prophesied, the Spaniards, once the handover had been completed, took no more interest in the islands, and it is only now, in the second half of the twentieth century, that Argentina has remembered old claims. Byron's settlers, however, held on, so that the islands became a British colony.

Finding that the *Étoile*, his supply ship, had not arrived at Fort St Louis. Bougainville was in a quandary. He was short of supplies and would not venture into the Pacific without a supply ship. The *Boudeuse*, a frigate, did not have sufficient room for provisions—unlike the converted collier in which Captain Cook made his lone voyage into the same seas. Throughout the months of April and May, therefore, Bougainville remained in the Falklands awaiting the *Étoile*; but, at last, despairing of her arrival, he decided to start for Rio de Janeiro, where, he had arranged with de la Giraudais (commander of the *Étoile*), the two ships were to meet up if prevented from meeting at the Falklands.

On 2 June he made up his mind to leave the by-then almost deserted islands. He records, "it was with a sorrowful heart, that I bade farewell to the little islands where I had sown the seeds of so many hopes". On 21 December he entered the harbour of Rio de Janeiro, where he had the satisfaction of seeing the *Étoile* lying at anchor. (Commerson places this event six days later.) De la Giraudais explained the reason for his delay. He had not been able to leave Rochefort until February, three whole months after the date fixed. After crossing the Atlantic he had found his fresh-water butts leaking, the masts and rigging in urgent need of repair, and the ship in need of recaulking. He had therefore been obliged to put in at Montevideo. There he learned of Bougainville's movements, and, fearing that he would miss him if he continued to the Falklands, decided to head for Rio.

On board the *Étoile* were the renowned botanist Philibert Commerson, whom the Duc de Praslin had appointed official naturalist to the expedition; a surgeon from Rochefort by the name of Vivés; and a young astronomer, Pierre-Antoine Veron. At a later date Bougainville had Veron transferred to the *Boudeuse* as pilot–observer, to carry out experiments in the new method of calculating longitude.

Once more there were delays before the expedition could proceed on its way. Although the *Étoile* carried salted provisions and drinking water to last thirteen months, her supplies of bread were clearly insufficient. As in Rio, neither biscuit, wheat nor flour was to be obtained. It was therefore thought necessary to return to Montevideo to obtain these commodities. Meanwhile, in Rio, three weeks were spent in carrying out repairs and in taking aboard large supplies of timber.

These three weeks were full of incidents provoked by the disagreeable and uncertain temper of the Viceroy of Brazil, the Conde d'Acunha. The *Étoile's* paymaster was murdered and it was found impossible to get any redress; and the *Boudeuse*, on arriving at Rio, was not accorded the customary salute fired when a man o' war enters a friendly port. Bougainville sent the Chevalier de Bournand to interview the Conde d'Acunha about this lapse of good manners. In reply, the Viceroy merely replied that, if anybody met another person in the street, he took off his hat and did not trouble if this politeness was returned; but, if the French saluted the place, he would know what course to pursue. "If the *Boudeuse* fires a salute, I shall consider what my own position would be." These, according to Commerson, were his actual words. Bougainville refused to regard this as an answer, and did not order a salute. Nevertheless he records,

> On the 22nd we went in a body to pay a formal visit to the Viceroy. He returned this visit on the 25th, and upon his departure we fired a salute of nineteen guns, which was returned by the land battery.
>
> During this visit he offered us every assistance in his power: he even gave me permission to buy a corvette, which would have been of great use during our expedition, and he assured me that he would find out those who had murdered the paymaster of the *Étoile* . . . and get them punished. So he promised; but the rights of man have no influence here. Yet the Viceroy's kind attention was maintained for several days. He announced that he would arrange a *petit souper* for us, close to the seashore, in a garden full of jasmine and oranges; and he even gave us a box at the opera. There we were able to see the *chefs d'œuvres* of Metastasio performed by a troupe of mulattos and we were allowed to hear the masterpieces of great Italian composers interpreted by a bad orchestra, conducted by a hump-backed priest, dressed in his ecclesiastical garments!
>
> All the Spaniards and other residents were astonished at the favours showered on us, but warned us that it would not continue; in particular, a Spanish captain who had put in for repairs was treated with the utmost discourtesy.

It is clear that these residents knew the Viceroy well, for very soon his behaviour became quite impossible. He refused to allow delivery of the boat that Bougainville had bought; he refused the French permission to cut wood, or even to lodge on shore in a house that they had hired for the purpose. Bougainville called on him, to remonstrate, but d'Acunha gave him no time to speak. Bougainville records,

> On the first words that I said, he stood up in a fury, ordered me to leave the palace and, no doubt annoyed because I and my two officers remained seated in spite of his rage, called for his guard. But his guard, being more prudent than himself, did not appear and we retired

without the slightest sign of excitement on the part of anybody. As soon as we had gone he doubled the palace guard, reinforced the palace controls and issued orders to arrest any Frenchmen found in the streets after sunset.

Commerson, however, either was specially favoured by the Viceroy or simply paid no attention to his orders, for with his faithful servant Baret (or Baré) he wandered far and wide, his servant laden with specimens of all sorts. He wrote to a friend,

> This country is the loveliest in the world. In the very middle of winter, oranges, bananas and pineapples continually succeed each one another; the trees never lose their greenery; the interior, rich in every sort of game, as well as in sugar, rice, manioc, and so on, offers without any labour or cultivation a delicious subsistence, which is enjoyed also by thousands of slaves, who have but the trouble of gathering its fruits. . . .
>
> You know my mania for observing everything; in the midst of all these troubles, in spite of formal prohibition to go outside the town, and even notwithstanding a fearful sore on my leg which appeared at sea, I ventured to go out twenty times with my servant in a canoe, which was paddled by two blacks, and visited one after another the different shores and islands of the bay.

Bougainville, on learning from his surgeon that Commerson was in danger of losing his leg from gangrene, put him under arrest, although in the most friendly way, until his "fearful sore" should be healed. At Rio, Commerson might well have joined the *Boudeuse*, but, because he would not have had as much room there, preferred to remain aboard the *Étoile*, with his instruments, his books and his herbarium, even though the ship's company of the *Étoile* were on the whole a much rougher lot than their comrades on the frigate. De la Giraudais was no doubt exceptional, for he later gave up his more commodious quarters to the botanist and his servant; moreover, Commerson was often invited to dine at the tables of the élite of Rio, and was even invited to the viceregal palace, which aroused great jealousy.

It was while exploring in the neighbourhood of Rio that Commerson discovered the exquisite climbing plant to which he gave the name "Bougainvilia". Bougainville, one may be sure, was delighted by this courteous gesture, for his taste for action never excluded him from a delicate appreciation of the attractions of nature. Similarly to Commerson, he wrote in his Journal,

> nothing could be finer than the views of the countryside that greet the eye whatever way one turns; and we should have been glad indeed to have seen more of this charming country. Its inhabitants had expressed

to us in the frankest way the displeasure that they felt at the unfriendly treatment meted out to us by their Viceroy, while for our part we were only sorry that we were unable to remain for a longer time among them.

On 15 July 1767, still without adequate supplies of timber and of other commodities that the Viceroy had once so generously offered them, the *Boudeuse* and the *Étoile* glided out of the harbour of Rio de Janeiro on a perfectly calm sea.

Chapter Four

The Jesuits

On 31 July, a fortnight after their departure from Rio de Janeiro, the *Boudeuse* and the *Étoile* were once again at anchor in the bay of Montevideo. Bougainville planned to stay there no longer than six weeks—that is to say, until the change of the equinox, and just long enough to take on wood and provisions and carry out the usual servicing—but the *Étoile* suffered serious damage when she was accidentally rammed by another vessel. She had to be unloaded, her masts had to be replaced and her bowsprit needed refitting. This operation was impossible to carry out in Montevideo and it was recommended that she should be towed up river to Baragan, where the necessary repairs could be effected. Bougainville himself carried out this difficult navigation. On arrival at Baragan, as he records in his Journal, he was most unimpressed by the appearance of the town. "There were no shops on shore", he wrote, "and only a few houses, or huts rather, built of rushes overlaid with leather, scattered here and there on a sunbaked soil, and inhabited by people who know no other happiness than idleness."

Most of the French officers soon left this inhospitable township and took up quarters in Montevideo, where they established a hospital. They had plenty of time on their hands and with the dashing Prince of Nassau-Siegen made expeditions into the neighbouring pampas on horseback and took part in some thrilling, often dangerous jaguar hunts. As for Bougainville, his activity knew no bounds. His relationship with Governor-General Bucarelli was far more cordial than his dealings with the Viceroy of Brazil had been.

It was now that there occurred an event of capital importance which particularly attracted Bougainville's and Commerson's attention. This was the expulsion of the Jesuits, by order of the King of Spain, from all the Spanish colonies in South America, and the confiscation of their property. As became a man of the eighteenth century, everything concerning the life of a nation or the evolution of its people was of profound interest to Bougainville; he concerned himself with all the great movements of humanity, and in this case he carried out exhaustive research into the causes of the upheaval, of which he was an impartial witness, and about which he wrote in a manner distinguished by remarkable vitality and picturesqueness. At the close of the sixteenth century the Jesuits had begun to found missions on the fertile shores of the Paraná and the Uruguay; these priests, who were as able as they were learned, had been ordered by the King of Spain to preach the faith to the Indians. As Bougainville put it,

> Two motives, religion and interest—which monarchs are privileged to combine when there is no danger, lest the one should prejudice the other—had made the Spanish sovereign anxious for the conversion of the Indians; because, by their baptism as Catholics, savages were turned into civilized human beings; and because at the same time this ensured mastery over a vast and luxuriant country. Thus a new source of wealth was opened up to the mother country, and new recruits were gained to swell the ranks of worshippers of the true God.

At first, as Bougainville avers, the Jesuits applied themselves with every discretion to the difficult task with which they had been entrusted, confining themselves to softening the rude disposition of the Indians by argument and by preaching.

> The Jesuits embarked on their mission with the courage of martyrs and a patience that was truly angelic. Both the one and the other were needed—to attract, and to hold when attracted, to break to obedience and to persuade to work, a race of men as violent as they were fickle, and as wedded to their idleness as to their independence. The obstacles were without number, and difficulties arose at every step; but zeal triumphed and the gentleness of the missionaries at length brought these wild inhabitants of the forest to their feet. They gathered them into communities, accustomed them to living in houses, drew up a code of laws for them, instructed them in useful and ornamental arts; in fact, from a barbarous nation, devoid of morals and religion, they created a docile, orderly people, punctilious in the observance of Christian ceremonies. The Indians, won over by the persuasive eloquence of their teachers, were glad to obey men whom they found ever ready to sacrifice themselves for the happiness of others; and so well did they learn their lesson that, when they wished to form an idea of the King of Spain, they thought of him as apparelled in the habit of St Ignatius.

Little by little, with great moderation and prudence, the Jesuits progressed from spiritual to temporal domination. Each tribe was governed by two Jesuits: one, with the title of curé (vicar), being placed in charge of material interests, the other, known as the vice-curé and subordinate to the first, attending to spiritual matters. Indians of every age and both sexes were compelled to work for the good of the community and of the tribe at large, while the curé gathered into store the fruits of their collective labours and made himself responsible for the feeding and clothing of all. The Jesuits had given material form, in part at least, to Jean-Jacques Rousseau's dreams of social equality. Every Indian was the equal of his brother, and none was allowed to own private property. Bougainville could not help admiring the marvellous gift for teaching and powers of organization which blessed these disciples of Ignatius Loyola, who, both in Paraguay and in Uruguay, by the influence of their word alone, without the help of any armed force and without money, had converted hundreds of thousands of wild and wandering savages to the Christian faith, and persuaded them to work and unquestioning obedience.

> I should be inclined [he wrote] to instance the methods of government practised by these missionaries as the model of an administration destined to bring happiness and wisdom to humanity. Indeed, when one reviews as a whole and from a distant standpoint this wonderous government, founded solely by the force of spiritual arms, and bound only by the chains of persuasion, what institution more honourable to mankind could one's imagination conjure up? Here is a society, inhabiting a fertile country and enjoying a favourable climate, in which all the members are workers and each individual labours in the common cause, the fruits of their joint efforts being scrupulously handed over for keeping in public-storehouses, whence each is provided with all that is needful for his sustenance, his clothing and the upkeep of his household. The adult supports the newly-born child by his efforts, and when with the years his vigour fails him he receives at the hands of his fellow-citizens the self-same services which in times past he had rendered to them. The houses are well-planned, the public buildings handsome; the creed is uniform and strictly observed; and this happy people know neither rank nor position, and are preserved equally from the snares of riches as from the spectre of want. So should have appeared to me, and so actually did appear, and with the enchantment that distance lends, the achievement of the missionaries. . . .

More strict inquiry, the testimony of numerous witnesses, the evidence of facts, all helped somewhat to lessen Bougainville's initial enthusiasm for the ideal government of the Jesuits.

> With such slavish submission did the Indians defer to the authority of their priests that not only did they allow themselves, men and women alike, to be flogged, as in the schools of today, for public transgressions, but they even went so far as themselves to solicit

chastisement for their moral faults. Every year, in each parish, the Fathers elected *corregidores* [magistrates] and *capitulaires* [Jesuit canons] charged with the various duties of the administration . . . the elected prostrating themselves at the feet of the curé to receive the insignia of their office, which, be it said, did not exempt them, if occasion arose, from a flogging along with the rest. The chief outward mark of distinction granted these officials was the wearing of ecclesiastical robes; while a cotton shirt formed the only garment worn by the rest of the Indians, of either sex. . . . From eight o'clock in the morning the people were scattered at their various tasks, either in the fields or in the workshops, and the *corregidores* took care to see that not a second of time was wasted. Every Monday a certain quantity of raw cotton for spinning was distributed among the women, and this they had to return, at the end of the week, woven into cloth. At 5.30 every evening they collected to recite together the rosary, and to kiss once more the hand of the curé, a ceremony which they had already once performed at seven o'clock in the morning. Then followed the distribution of an ounce of *maté* [a herb tea] and four pounds of beef for each household, reckoned as consisting of eight persons, and maize was also served out. On Sunday, when there was no work, divine service took up even more of their time, but after this was over they were free to indulge in recreation, and to play games, the dullness of which could only be compared to the dreariness of their lives. One may see by these details that the Indians possessed no individual property of any kind, and that they were subjected to a cruelly tedious routine of work and play. This ennui, so rightly called "mortal", is explanation enough of the well-known fact that they passed out of this life without regret, and died without ever having really lived. When once they fell ill, it was but rarely they recovered, and when asked if they looked on death as a misfortune, they answered "No", and answered it with a conviction that left no doubt of their sincerity. . . . For the rest, the Jesuits represented these Indians to us as a race incapable of attaining a higher degree of intelligence than that of children, and the lives these big children led prevented them from sharing the gaiety of little ones.

Excepting their participation, in 1757, in an insignificant revolt against Spanish rule (which insurrection was rapidly quelled, at the expense of some bloodshed), the Indians proved the most docile of subjects and the Spanish Court could only congratulate itself on having confided to the Society of Jesus the task of subjugating them.

However, there came a time when a wave of hatred against the Jesuits swept through Europe. In 1764 Louis XV drove them out of France; Portugal persecuted and expelled them; and, actuated by no particular motive and without any preliminary inquiry, in April 1767 Charles II of Spain ordered the arrest of all Jesuits in Spain and issued a decree abolishing the Society. In June of the same year, in Buenos Aires, Governor-General Bucarelli received orders to arrest and deport all Jesuits working on the missions within his jurisdiction. The task was a difficult one and, in order to avoid the risk of a rising by the Indians, had to be carried out with the utmost secrecy; but its execution was a triumph of tact and efficiency. When it is a question of destroying something, mankind discovers itself to be capable of unlimited organization. As a first step, Bucarelli circulated a despatch calling upon the missions to send him a *corregidor* and a *cacique* (headman) from each tribe, in order that he might communicate to them letters received from the King. It was essential that the Indians should be on their way to him and beyond the reach of the priests when news of the order of expulsion reached the missions. "By this means," noted Bougainville, "the Governor fulfilled two objects: on the one hand he secured hostages who ensured him the allegiance of the tribes when it came to the expulsion of the Jesuits; on the other hand he placed himself in a position to regain the affection of the Indians by reason of the good treatment that would be lavished upon them at Buenos Aires." The Jesuits viewed this general assembly of the Indian chiefs with no little apprehension: they had instructed them before their departure as to the lines of conduct they should observe, and had urged them to place no confidence in what the Governor might say to them: "Be ready, my children" they added, "to hear a great many lies."

On 13 September 120 *corregidores* and *caciques*, representing the various tribes that were subject to the missions, rode into Buenos Aires. On the way they had heard news of the expulsion of the Jesuits; but they had nevertheless continued their journey. Bougainville, who was present at the reception accorded them by the Governor, recounted the incident as follows:

> The Governor appeared on the balcony of the palace, and through his interpreters he made them welcome and told them that they might go away and rest themselves. He would, he said, inform them later as to the day on which he would be ready to tell them of the King's wishes. He added briefly that he had just delivered them from slavery and placed them once more in possession of their property, which up to the present they had not been permitted to enjoy. A loud shout greeted the Governor's words, and the Indians, with their right hands raised to heaven, united in wishing prosperity to the King and to the Governor. They showed no visible sign of discontent, but it was easy to trace more surprise than pleasure in the expression of their faces.

Bougainville, who never missed an opportunity of studying the habits of savages at close quarters, paid them a number of visits at this time, and summarized his impressions with his usual precision:

They struck me as being of an indolent nature; and they had, I noticed, that stupid expression which is so typical of trapped animals. I had been told that they had the reputation of being well informed, but as they spoke only the Guarani language, I was unable to gain any idea of the degree of their understanding. I did, however, hear a *cacique* who, I was assured, was a great musician, play the violin: he played a sonata, and I thought I was listening to the forced notes of a bird-organ.

The King's orders were executed, without a hitch, in every town in the colony, the Jesuit fathers offering little resistance. "They showed", remarked Bougainville, "the most perfect resignation, humbling themselves beneath the hand which struck them, and recognizing, as they said, that their sins deserved the punishment with which God had seen fit to afflict them." They were embarked for Europe, and by the irony of fate one of the first of the vessels by which they sailed for more hospitable regions was called the *Venus*.

Such was the history of the expulsion of the Jesuits, by order of His Most Catholic Majesty, from the Spanish colonies of South America. Bougainville later referred to these events, of which chance had made him a witness, as forming one of the most interesting episodes in the course of his long voyage.

His final judgement on the Jesuits was that of a commonsense man whose mind was untainted by hatred and passion (Commerson, by contrast, was not so generous in his opinion of the Society, and makes some truly absurd indictments):

> My pen refuses to lend itself to the chronicling of all that the public of Buenos Aires claims to have discovered in papers seized from the Jesuits [in fact, no such papers were found]: animosities are still too recent to enable one to distinguish the false accusations from the true. *I prefer to do justice to the majority of those members of this Society of Jesus, who took no part in nor had any knowledge of its temporal ambitions. Some intriguers there may well have been among so large a body, but the monks for the most part were a truly religious set of men, who saw in the institution only the piety of its founder, and served both in the spirit and in the letter the God to whom they had been consecrated.* [Emphasis added.]

Chapter Five

The Straits of Magellan

The crews of the *Boudeuse* and the *Étoile* spent some happy days on the shores of the river Plate. The food was excellent—particularly by comparison with the monotonous diet of salted provisions to which they had been accustomed at sea. Now they could feed on fresh meat, vegetables and fruit to their heart's content. It was a source of particular satisfaction to Bougainville that his men were all in such excellent health, a most exceptional occurrence in the days of sail, when scurvy took such a heavy toll of seamen. Hygiene was always of prime importance on all vessels under his command.

But the time of departure was approaching and fresh provisions sufficient for a ten-month voyage were taken aboard. When the roll was called, twelve men—soldiers and sailors—were missing, deserters who preferred the sunny skies of La Plata and the caresses of the brown-skinned ladies of Spain to the certain hardships of a lengthy journey. To add to this defection Bougainville was obliged to leave behind the master-pilot, as well as the master-armourer and a petty officer of the *Boudeuse*, "whose age and incurable infirmities would not", he said, "allow them to undertake the voyage". The shortage of personnel caused by the loss of these men was, however, soon made good, for in the Falkland Islands Bougainville had taken on board several seafaring fishermen, as well as an engineer and an officer of the merchant service, all of whom, experienced men, volunteered to fill the deficiencies.

All was now ready. On 14 November, under a light north-easterly breeze, the *Boudeuse* and the *Étoile* put out from Montevideo harbour for the great unknown. Bougainville decided to navigate the Straits of Magellan, which were known to Alexandre Duclos-Guyot, and had in part been explored by the *Aigle* in 1764. Although this route was long and dangerous, the route round Cape Horn had the reputation of being even more perilous.

A few days out of the river Plate, the vessels ran into tremendous seas. Again, all the livestock taken aboard at Montevideo perished. Poor Philibert Commerson, the botanist, was excruciatingly ill—so racked with stomach pains and nausea that he believed himself to be at death's door. It was fortunate for him that he had brought with him his faithful servant Baret, who shared his cabin and lavished the most devoted care on him.

After sailing for a fortnight under appalling weather conditions, the two ships reached Cape Virgin, which marks the eastern entrance to the Straits of Magellan, which they succeeded in entering only after many difficulties. During the night of 7 December, they observed fires burning on the Patagonian coast, on the shores of what was to be called Possession Bay. Next day they noticed that a white flag had been hoisted on an eminence near the sea. "These Patagonians", wrote Bougainville, "were doubtless the same as those with whom the crew of the *Étoile* had had dealings in the bay of Boucault on its first visit in search of wood, and the flag they displayed was the one given to them as a token of friendship by Denys de St-Simon. The care with which they had preserved it was a sign that they were a gentle people, faithful to their word and grateful for the gifts bestowed on them."

On the southern side of the straits, on Tierra del Fuego, appeared a score or so of natives dressed in skins, running as fast as possible in an effort to keep pace with the vessels, and making friendly gestures. Bougainville decided to anchor in Possession Bay and put ashore with some of his officers (including Commerson, who was now fully restored to health). Scarcely had they landed when they saw six mounted Patagonians approaching them at full gallop. When the natives were about sixteen yards distant, they dismounted with cries of what sounded like "Chaoua!" and rushed headlong towards the strangers. They seemed delighted at the sight of the white men, and grasped their hands and embraced them with every sign of affection. These manifestations of amity were accompanied by the chanting of the word *chaoua*, which, as Bougainville wrote, appeared to be some sort of Patagonian equivalent of the Te Deum. Fresh bread and biscuit were brought from the boats and distributed among these friendly people, whose numbers were increasing with every minute and who did full justice to the fare provided. Then began the business of barter. Vicuña skins and those of other animals were exchanged for trifling trinkets, beads and suchlike, which to the natives' unaccustomed eyes had great value. They then made signs that they would like to have some tobacco. Each was given a large nip of brandy, "and as soon as they had swallowed it", Bougainville records, "they struck their throats with their hands and uttered trembling and inarticulate sounds, which ended in a rapturous smacking of the lips. Everyone behaved in the same manner and we were much struck by their strange behaviour."

Commerson and some of the officers then set out to look for plants, accompanied by several Patagonians. One of the natives seemed particularly attached to the distinguished naturalist, or, rather, to his blue frock-coat. By means of gestures he made it clear that he would willingly exchange the coat for his daughter in marriage, an offer which Commerson tactfully declined.

At sunset the French returned to their boats, escorted to the water's edge by their Patagonian friends, who took possession of everything they could lay

hands on. After a final "Chaoua!", to which the French heartily responded, the
natives made off at full gallop.

> These natives [wrote Bougainville in his Journal] are the same as those
> encountered by the *Étoile* in 1766. . . . The men are of fine stature:
> among those we met with, none was less than five feet six inches, or
> more than five feet nine or ten inches, tall; but on the preceding
> voyage the crew of the *Étoile* had seen several who were as much as
> six feet tall. What struck me as phenomenal was the huge breadth of
> their shoulders, the size of their heads and the thickness of their limbs.
> They are robust and well nourished, their muscles taut, their flesh firm
> and compact. Here is a race living close to nature, nourishing itself on
> food rich in sugar, [a race] that has developed as fully as it is capable of
> doing. Their countenances are neither hard nor disagreeable and some-
> times they might be described as handsome; their faces are rather round
> and flat, their eyes bright, and in Paris the only defect from which
> their teeth, which are extremely white, would be thought to suffer is
> that of being somewhat too large. They have long black hair, which
> they wear coiled on the tops of their heads. I saw some with mous-
> taches, which made up in length what they lacked in thickness. In
> colour they are bronze, as are all the natives of America, whether
> living in the torrid zone or in the temperate or arctic regions.
> Although a few had their faces painted red, there was nothing else
> about them that suggested savagery.

Bougainville then describes their weapons, similar to those used by the horsemen of the plains of La Plata, but including also knives of English manufacture—
probably, he suggests, given to them by Mr Byron. This seems highly unlikely,
as, when he passed through the straits, Byron was a mere boy and a midshipman.
No doubt Anson, who had been commander of the expedition, had presented
the knives.

"Their principal food", continues Bougainville, "seemed to be the marrow
and flesh of the guanaco [a sort of red-coated llama]. Some of them carried large
pieces of raw meat attached to their saddles, from which we saw them take a
mouthful from time to time."

He tells us that their horses were emaciated and always followed by a pack
of small and ugly dogs. Both dogs and horses drank sea water, fresh water being
very rare along the coast and even inland.

Of the social organization of the natives he writes,

> I believe that no single one of them was possessed individually of any
> more influence or prestige than the other. . . . I believe these people
> live the same life as Tartars, wandering over the immense plains of

South America, always in the saddle, men, women and children alike, hunting the game or cattle in which the country abounds, clothing themselves and fashioning their shelters from the same source. . . .

The *Boudeuse* and the *Étoile* continued on their way, encountering a thousand difficulties and delays, for the straits are 375 miles in length and no more than twelve to seventeen wide; a strong current runs through them and westerly gales are prevalent. The weather was found most changeable, as Veron explains:

> in the space of a few moments the skies would change from the clearest blue to a threatening grey, and the calm of a Mediterranean spring would give place to rain. Tacking incessantly the *Boudeuse* made slow progress, skirted on the north by the wooded shores of Patagonia, while to the south, on the coast line of Tierra del Fuego, rose sinister mountains covered with snow as ancient as the world.

After putting in at a small island which the *Aigle* had named St Elizabeth, where there was nothing but a small lake of brackish water and a few bustards, Bougainville continued on his way. Although the most difficult part of the straits was behind them, the *Boudeuse* and *Étoile* were soon to find themselves among some of the most inhospitable shores to be found. On the 16th they moved on to Bouchage (or Bournand) bay, where Commerson, in spite of every conceivable difficulty—storm, rain, snow, almost impassable forests, spongy peat and rugged ravines—obtained new and interesting plants for his herbarium. Indeed, his cabin was becoming far too small to accommodate his collection, and it was now that de la Giraudais, the captain, allowed him to take over his own more spacious quarters.

On 17 December the vessels doubled the most southerly point of the South American mainland and anchored in the small bay that the crew of the *Aigle*, who in 1765 had collected wood there for the Falklands, had named after Bougainville. Bougainville decided to establish a camp on shore and to stay till the end of the month, loading fresh supplies of water and wood. Commerson, with Baret and the Prince of Nassau-Siegen, at once departed for the woods to hunt and botanize. They found no wild animals, but brought back "snipe, teal duck and bustards and some *perruches* [perhaps sea parrots or penguins]".

On 6 January 1768 they received a visit from some of the natives of Tierra del Fuego. Commerson tells us that, unlike the Patagonians they had met earlier, "these savages are small, ugly, thin and smell abominably". For clothes they had nothing but a few badly-prepared sealskins. Their canoes were made of pieces of bark, tied together with rushes and caulked with moss. They were often moored to the seaweed or kelp, and their wretched women, who, he tells us, were hideous, had to swim out continually in the icy cold water to fetch them inshore.

Unfortunately, some of the crew gave a native boy a looking-glass, which he promptly broke. He ate some of it and thrust pieces up his nose. Despite every effort by the local "doctors" and the French, he died in agony and the natives fled. Bougainville was heartbroken.

Summing up his observations of the natives and the conditions in which they lived, he wrote in his Journal, "Deprived of everything that renders life agreeable, they [the natives] have to endure the most horrible climate in the world." His opinion of the climate received added confirmation when, on 16 January, when a temporary break in the weather offered a chance to leave the straits, the wind changed direction as the *Boudeuse* was trying to warp her way out. As a result, she fell away into shallow water and nearly foundered on the rocky shore. Her crew were lucky to be able to guide her back to a bay, previously visited, that they had named Port Galant; but there they suffered the worst hurricane they had so far experienced. The ships' anchors dragged and the men were obliged to put out their great cable and bring down their yards and topmasts.

Despite the ghastly weather, shrubs and plants were all in flower. However, Commerson wrote, "this did not avail to dissipate the sadness with which we had been affected by long continued observation of this dreadful country. The most frivolous character could not help but be downcast in this awful climate...." In another letter, to a doctor friend in Montpellier, he wrote, "We had twenty-four hours of daylight and scarcely any appearance of night. But one must imagine the most utter desolation in all Nature, which somehow here seems to be tired of producing mankind and of producing for its needs." Yet Commerson and Baret (and sometimes also the Prince) braved the conditions in further botanical researches.

Veron, the astronomer, prepared in vain to observe an eclipse of the moon. Ceaseless rain, on the night in question, prevented him from seeing anything.

By daylight, however, Bougainville and he made some useful surveys of the shores of the straits—preparing, for the benefit of seamen who would pass that way in the future, charts of the coastline, detailing bays, estuaries, safe anchorages and so on. The *Boudeuse*'s longboat was used in making these surveys, which were remarkably accurate.

Bougainville even climbed a mountain on Tierra del Fuego. From there he looked out on "a tangled conglomeration of islands, some large, some small, but all mountainous and of monstrous shape and with their summits covered with eternal snow".

On the night of the 23rd, after three days, of storms and hurricanes, the ships at last got away again. Unusually, a strong easterly wind blew up, dissipating a dense fog that had obscured all vision for some hours. The morning light revealed the *Boudeuse* and the *Étoile* moving freely through the shining

The author's painting of the island of Tahiti after a contemporary artist's reconstruction from descriptions by Bougainville and Captain Cook.

Michael Ross

waters of the Pacific Ocean with Cap Pilar and the Straits of Magellan well behind them. It had taken them fifty-two days to complete the journey through the straits, which an English navigator, Narborough, named the "Desolation of the South". "Indeed," wrote Bougainville, "anything more frightful it would be difficult to conceive."

Chapter Six

The Pacific—First Discoveries—Tahiti

The *Boudeuse* and the *Étoile* were now sailing on the vast, mysterious southern seas, of which so little was yet known. Bougainville ordered the two ships to separate during the day and rejoin each other at night, in order to allow the navigators to examine as great an area of the ocean as possible.

Bougainville had set a northwesterly course in search of Easter Island (sighted by the English filibuster Davis in 1606; its position was later confirmed by the Dutchman Roggeveen) and Pepys Island (which a Royal Navy officer, Captain Cowley, claimed to have discovered, but seems to have invented). Neither Davis nor Roggeveen, "for reasons of State", divulged the position of Easter Island.

For three weeks the *Boudeuse* and the *Étoile* were out of sight of land. Some of the crew fell sick from scurvy and sore throats but were soon put on their feet again. A more serious disaster occurred when one of the sailors fell overboard and, despite every effort to save him, was drowned. This was only the second casualty of its kind, for a cabin boy had suffered the same fate just after the *Boudeuse* had sailed from Nantes.

On 22 February, four islets and a small island were sighted on the horizon. These Bougainville named the Four Facardins, after a delightful story by Antony Hamilton, one of his favourite authors. Hamilton, almost forgotten now, was born in Ireland in 1646, but spent most of his life in France. According to *Chambers's Encyclopaedia*, "his writing is full of wit and talent, particularly his *Contes de Féerie* and his *Memoires du Comte de Grammont*". He died in France in 1720, a loyal supporter of the Stuart cause to the last.

The vessels sailed towards the little island, whose pleasant shores "seemed to invite the travellers to land there for good and all", wrote Bougainville. "The verdure charmed our eyes, and the coconut-palms everywhere offered us their fruits and their shade in glades adorned with flowers, while the thousands of birds fluttering about the shore revealed that there were plenty of fish; but, although we longed to go ashore, no anchorage could be found, and so, unhappily, we had to abandon the idea of landing."

Though the land may have been attractive enough, the same could not be said of its inhabitants, for some twenty naked savages appeared on the shore, brandishing long spears. This warlike demonstration caused Bougainville to name this particular place Île des Lanciers (Isle of the Lancers). Next day they encountered another little island, which because of its shape he named Harp island, but here again the inhabitants appeared unfriendly, and to land seemed bound to result in unnecessary loss of life. For several days thereafter, the *Boudeuse* and *Étoile* continued to navigate among low, partly submerged islands, which Bougainville christened the Dangerous Archipelago and altered course to avoid.

The journey was by no means uninteresting to Commerson, who was earnestly observing and dissecting fish. At times, flying fishes, like swarms of butterflies, hovered around or landed on the vessels—among them a new species, which was duly named *Exocaetus Commersonii*. Another beautiful new fish, remarkable for its brilliant colouring, preyed on them. There was also the Gold-tail dolphin, yet another genus hitherto unknown, which had a silvery white throat and breast and, excepting its blue fins and the blue spots on its back, seemed to be covered all over with shiny gold. These dolphins afforded excellent eating "when cooked with butter and capers".

On 2 April a high, steep mountain appeared in the distance, and was named Boudeuse Peak. On the night of 3–4 April, fires were seen burning on a neighbouring coast, which came clearly into view at break of day. Some canoes emerged from a bay and steered for the ships, then others shot out lightly from all parts of the island.

> One of these [writes Bougainville] preceded the others and was manned by twelve naked men who held up some banana leaves, making signs that these were intended as an emblem of peace. We replied with every sign of friendship we could think of, and one of them, whose thick hair stood out like a halo, offered us a little pig and a cluster of bananas. . . . We accepted his presents and in exchange gave him some caps and handkerchiefs. These first presents exchanged were the pledge of our friendship with these people.

As if by enchantment, the canoes increased in numbers until at least one hundred were gathered around the ships. The natives offered the Frenchmen coconuts, bananas and other exotic fruits, in exchange for nails and other trifles. All this bartering was carried out with the utmost good humour.

The inhabitants seemed so hospitable and the surroundings so agreeable that Bougainville decided to stay for a while.

> The coast, which rises like an amphitheatre [he wrote in his Journal], seems delightful in our eyes. Although the mountains are of considerable height, in no place is the bare rock visible, all the slopes being covered with trees. Scarcely could we believe our eyes when, in the

midst of the southern part of the isle, we found a peak clothed with
trees right up to its lonely summit, which shot up from the middle of
the range. From afar it looked like an immense pyramid, adorned by
the hand of a skilful architect with gardens of green foliage. The lower
parts of the country are intersected by meadows and groves, and at the
foot of the highlands the whole coast is edged with a strip of low-level
ground covered with vegetation. Here, in the midst of banana plantations, coconut-palms and other trees laden with fruits, we saw the
houses of the islanders, and, as we made our way along the coast, we
caught sight of a beautiful cascade bursting forth from the mountain-
side to hurl its foaming waters into the sea.

For two days the *Étoile* and *Boudeuse* coasted up and down the island in search of
a suitable anchorage. At last, on 6 April, a suitable bay was found, on the shores
of what proved to be none other than the divine island of Tahiti.

Even before the vessels dropped anchor, innumerable canoes had surrounded
them. The very friendly and businesslike natives brought quantities of
food, including chickens and pigeons, fishing tackle, stone axes and
bizarre-looking cloths. In exchange they asked for iron and—of all things—
earrings.

The French were much diverted by all this bustle and barter and only too
happy to take part in activities of which they had long been deprived. But one
can imagine their excitement when some canoes came alongside bearing
women, nearly all young, pretty and graceful and extremely friendly. Small
rush hats covered their fine heads, shielding their light brown faces. Their eyes
were velvety and their teeth of extreme whiteness. Like the men, most of them
were almost naked; but some wore thin, fluttering materials. "The sailors",
noted Bougainville, "were much excited at the sight of these well-proportioned
goddesses, whose figures had not been spoiled by years of discomfort." One
can be sure that Bougainville and his officers were no less affected. "Taio!"
("Friend!"), they all cried again and again. An islander came on board the
Étoile and spent the night there, afterwards expressing with eloquent gestures
the warm welcome he had received.

The Prince of Nassau-Siegen wrote, a little more explicitly, "one of the
islanders, full of confidence inspired by innocence, came on board with his wife
and asked for our friendship. His wife, showing willingly all the perfections of a
beautiful body, displayed all that was most enticing to win over the hearts of
the newcomers."

A few days later Fesche, former pilot of the *Aigle*, witnessed the following
scene.

One of the native bystanders obtained a flute, from which she drew sweet and agreeable sounds. A rug was brought to the spot, on which a young girl sat; signs from all the Indians made it clear what was expected of us. However, so contrary was this behaviour to what we were accustomed to that, to be reassured, one of us approached the proffered "victim" and gave her a false pearl, which he attached to her ear, and risked a kiss, which was returned with fervour. A bold hand, guided by love . . . slipped as if by chance over breasts still hidden by a veil, which was soon removed by the girl herself, whom we now saw clad in the only clothes worn by Eve before her sin.

She did more. She stretched herself out on the mat and struck the chest of her aggressor and made it clear that she was offering herself to him and spread apart the two obstacles which prevent the entrance into that temple to which so many men sacrifice their days. . . .

Unfortunately, her would-be lover, an expert with the foil, but unused to making love with fifty Indians looking on, *mis un frein à ses désirs violents* (put a brake on his violent desires). Who was the would-be lover? I wonder. The handsome young Prince? Fesche, only twenty-three years old, had never before seen anything like it. No wonder he recorded it in his Journal.

But perhaps it is Commerson who gives the most vivid description of the island. He was, of course, soon furiously busy, describing and dissecting new and rare fishes, or gathering the many new and strange plants never before seen by a botanist. Everywhere he found the most gorgeous colouring and vividly contrasting tints. Not only were there extraordinary parakeets in bright red and vivid blue plumage, and splendid blue pigeons, and charming little green turtledoves, but also, in the still and transparent waters of the lagoons, a whole paradise of marine life, strange and beautiful.

He found fish that were a brilliant blue all over (*Gomphosus caeruleus*), and others that were red, yellow and blue (*Gomphosus varius*). He found also the sea frog (so called), which has purple rims to its eyes, and long needle-like spines (which can be made to point in any direction) all over its back. A still stranger find was the toadfish, which covers itself with seaweeds and hides below rocks or burrows in the mud, in order to angle for impetuous fishes by means of the long filaments, beset with worm-like excrescences, that are attached to its muzzle. Its head is grotesquely horrible—especially its cuplike, mobile nostrils, which can be swivelled in the direction of any particularly strong smell. Fish of the *Scarus* genus (three new species) were found to have bony shagreened plates inside the mouth; these they use to crush madrepores and extract the animalcula from them.

No other circumnavigator of the world has ever contributed as much to natural history as Commerson did. It would require volumes to describe his discoveries (of which, unfortunately, many details were lost in the course of transportation back to France). Even Captain S. Pasfield Oliver's *Life of Philibert Commerson*, published by John Murray in 1909, has to pass over most of his discoveries. Commerson's notebooks are extremely technical and, Captain Pasfield Oliver avers, superior to those of Sir Joseph Banks (who participated in Cook's voyage round the world). Commerson, in writing to his friend Lalande, another great botanist, says,

> What presumption to lay down the law as to the number of plants and their characters in spite of all the discoveries which are yet to be made. Linnaeus only proposes some 7000 to 8000. . . . I venture to say however that I have already made by my own hand 25,000, and I am not afraid to declare that there exist at least four or five times as many species on the whole world's surface. . . .

"If Commerson had published his own observations, he would have been in the first rank of naturalists", wrote Cuvier. "Unfortunately he died before putting the final touch to his collections, and those to whom his herbaria and manuscripts were entrusted treated them in a most culpable manner. . . ."

But to return to Tahiti.

The French sailors found the Tahitian girls even less strictly virtuous than those of Spanish America. This interlude of promiscuous lovemaking (for such it was) in the shade of fruit and palm trees, and without even those abominable insects, so usual in the tropics, to mar their enjoyment, convinced them that this was an earthly paradise and a real Utopia.

It was Commerson who called it a real Utopia—the name, he explains, "that Thomas More gave to his ideal republic, deriving it from the Greek [for 'no place']". A life at sea of unutterable boredom, varied by scurvy, famine, and moments of extreme peril (both before and after their stay at Tahiti) must be held to excuse the rather highly coloured picture that he draws of the island:

> I can assure you that it is the one spot upon the earth's surface which is inhabited by men without vices, prejudices, wants, or dissensions. Born under the loveliest of skies, they are supported by the fruits of a soil so fertile that cultivation is scarcely required, and they are governed rather by a sort of family father than by a monarch. [In fact, as Cook discovered in the following year, they were ruled by a Queen.]
>
> They recognize no other god save Love. Every day is consecrated to him, and the whole island is his temple. . . .
>
> The women are meet rivals of the Georgians in beauty; they are sisters of the Graces, and entirely without clothing. . . .

He described with such enthusiasm and in such exceedingly vivid terms both the extent and the publicity of their love-making that his publishers refrained from printing this portion of his manuscript. He was not mistaken when he wrote,

> Some blighting censor might discover in all this nothing but de-bauchery, horrible prostitution, and the most shameless cynicism; but he would grossly deceive himself, failing to recognize the condition of the Natural Man, born essentially good, tainted by no prejudice, and following without mistrust and without remorse the sweet impulses of his instincts, always sure guides, for they have not yet degenerated into reasons.
>
> Their mother tongue, very sonorous and full of harmony, is made up of some four or five hundred words, which can neither be parsed nor conjugated (that is to say, with no grammar); it yet suffices to explain every idea, and to express all their desires: this magnificent simplicity, which does not forbid either modulation in tone or the pantomime of passion, secures them against that unconscionable bathology described by us as "the richness of language", and which causes us to lose, in a labyrinth of phrases, clear neatness of recognition and promptness of judgement.
>
> The Utopian, on the contrary, will name anything as soon as he observes it, and the very tone with which he pronounces it already explains the way in which it impresses him; few words produce rapid conversation; the soul's instincts, the heart's emotions, keep pace with the movements of the lips: speaker and hearer are always in accord with one another. . . .
>
> One must be careful not to entertain such a suspicion as that one is dealing only with a horde of gross and stupid savages. Everything in their homes manifests the greatest intelligence: as regards their canoes, they are constructed on entirely unknown lines; their navigation is directed by observation of the stars; their houses are large, elegant in shape, both comfortable and symmetrical; they have the art, not of weaving their cloth thread by thread, but of suddenly producing the fabric, entirely finished, simply by the blows of a mallet [perhaps barkcloth from paper mulberry, or from some sort of *Ficus*] . . . their fruit-trees are so planted at judicious intervals that they have not the tiresome monotony of our orchards, though retaining all that is agreeable and pleasant in the latter; the dangers of the coastline are marked by beacons, and are lighted at night for the sake of those at sea; they know all their plants, distinguishing them by names, and these names even explain their affinities and relationships; although the various tools employed in their arts are made of raw materials, yet, so far as regards the shape selected and certainty in operation, they can be compared even with our own. For these things they surely

deserve our respect, although our intercourse with them endured but
for a short period.

They were using iron before our visit; and how industriously they
worked this metal, exceedingly precious to them, and which they
employed only for really useful purposes! We ourselves have made it
a villainous substance by manufacturing from it the ordinary weapons
of murder and of despair.

Did they not refuse, horrified, the knives and daggers which we
offered them, seeming to divine instinctively the abuses that we had
committed with such implements? On the contrary, how eagerly
they came to examine and to take the dimensions of boats, sails, tents,
barrels, and indeed of everything which they supposed could be
imitated with advantage to themselves!

Then the simplicity of their moral code: the fairness of their treatment of women, who are in no way oppressed, as is the case with most
savages; their brotherly love to each other; their horror at the shedding
of man's blood; their deep veneration for the dead, who are supposed
to be only sleeping; their hospitality to strangers.[5] As regards all these
virtues, one must allow the journals the privilege of description, but
only in such terms as our gratitude and our admiration should require
of them.

Their chiefs were admitted to our tables. Everything that appeared
there excited their curiosity: they wanted an explanation of every
dish; if any vegetable seemed good, they asked for the seed of it, and,
on receiving some, wanted to know where and how it should be
planted, and when it would be ready for use. Our bread seemed
excellent to them, but we had to show them the corn of which it was
made, the way in which it was ground, and also our methods of fer-
menting and of baking.

They followed and understood all the details of these matters.
Indeed, often it was only necessary to tell them the half of it, for they
understood or divined the rest.

They had an invincible aversion to wine and spirits. Prudent in all
matters, they accept with faith both meat and drink straight from the
hands of Nature; neither fermented liquors nor cooking-pots are to be
found in their houses, and so nobody ever saw such beautiful teeth or
lips of so rich a red.

Both Bougainville and Commerson were much puzzled about how the Tahitians got to their island. Commerson, however, after a few preliminary remarks,
said that he could see no reason "why our good Tahitians should not be real
sons of the soil; I mean descended from Tahitian ancestors, and going as far
back as any nation, however jealous of its antiquity."

This suggestion, he said, was made "without prejudice" and because he knew of no nation with the slightest affinity to them in either morals, customs or language. He did, however, mention four or five words that seemed clearly Spanish in origin: *haourri*, like *hierro*, meaning "iron"; and *matao* or *matté*, meaning "killed" or "to kill" (Spanish *matar*). Could it be that some Spaniards were shipwrecked on the island, and gave the local language a word for "kill" by committing crimes previously unknown there?

Can it then be that the Tahitian language is distinguished, and indeed glorious, by having no native word whatever to express the idea of murder? So it was that the ancient law in Sparta had no penalties for parricide, because the Spartans could not conceive the possibility of it.

Unfortunately for Commerson's theory, the Tahitians, as he, though apparently not Bougainville, was unaware, practised human sacrifice and were constantly at war with neighbouring islands. As regards the etymological suggestion that Spaniards introduced iron to Tahiti, it was a British expedition, led by Captain Wallis, that had done so. Wallis's ship the *Dolphin* had called at Tahiti as recently as 1767.

Commerson mentions several arts and utensils that it seemed to him must have been introduced by the early Spanish navigators. He also gives them credit for introducing dogs and swine to the island. Modern archaeologists, however, have found that some of the things that Commerson points to as "Spanish" were known in Tahiti before they spread through prehistoric Europe. From these early times date lancets made of shell (for tattooing), earrings and bracelets, axes in the shape of an adze, and fishing lines and baskets.

Commerson makes a particular point of defending Tahitian ideas on property:

> I will not leave my dear Tahitians before I have absolved them from the atrocious accusation that they are mere thieving pickpockets. It is true that they did take many things from us, and that with a light-fingered dexterity which would have done credit to the most expert Parisian rascal.
>
> But should they be called thieves for this? What constitutes robbery?
>
> It is the taking of something which is the property of another person. The latter can only justly complain of being robbed if his proprietary right in the thing stolen has been established.
>
> But, as to this proprietary right, does it exist in a state of nature? No! It is a mere convention. Now, no convention can be considered binding unless it is generally known and recognized.
>
> But the Tahitian has no property of his own; he offers and generously presents anything as soon as he sees that some one wishes for it, and therefore has never recognized any exclusive proprietary right.

Therefore his action, in carrying off something belonging to you which has excited his curiosity, is only, in his eyes, an act of natural equity, by which he gives you to understand that you should behave towards him in the same way. I see no shadow of robbery in this!

Our Tahitian chief was an amusing rogue. He would pick up anything—a nail, a glass, or a biscuit—but would at once give it to the first of his people whom he met, taking from them pigs, chickens, or bananas, which he brought to us. Once I saw an officer lift his stick to him when he had been stealing after this fashion, of which we knew the generous motive. I immediately threw myself indignantly between them, at the risk of receiving the blow myself.

The Tahitian chief mentioned by Commerson was named Ereti. He invited Bougainville and his companions to an open-air repast outside his house, in which pleasant setting a banquet of fruits, grilled fish and clear fresh water was set before them. Garlands of rushes covered with black feathers and sharks' teeth were hung around the necks of Bougainville and the Chevalier d'Oraison.

On the following day Ereti arrived on board bringing a pig, some fowls and returning a pistol which had mysteriously been filched from one of the French officers.

However, when he and his council observed the French making preparations to establish a camp and a hospital on the island, close to the shore, Ereti showed a certain displeasure. He explained that the French "were free to come on land at their pleasure during the day, but at night should return to sleep on their vessels". Bougainville insisted on the establishment of the camp and emphasized that "it was necessary in order to facilitate the barter which was taking place between the two nations". A second council was then held, after which Ereti asked Bougainville if he intended to stay in the island always. With the aid of pebbles, the French commander explained that his visit would last only eighteen days. Yet another conference was held, during which time stones were placed before Bougainville, who continued to hold out for his eighteen. No animosity was shown on either side, and everything was finally settled to the satisfaction of the French: ". . . and joy prevailed once more", wrote Bougainville. Ereti even offered the French the use of a large shelter close to the river. There Bougainville had tents erected for the thirty-four of his men who had fallen victim to scurvy—strange in a country so full of vegetables and fresh meat. Perhaps Bougainville's surgeon was wrong in his diagnosis, but it is more likely that the men in question had suffered the illness during the passage through the Magellan Straits, and had not fully recovered, or, more probably, that they had contracted the sickness in the Pacific, where, before they reached Tahiti, conditions had been particularly bad.

A guard was placed on the hospital—a most necessary precaution to prevent admiring crowds from entering the great shed. Bougainville spent his first night on shore with Ereti, who wished to know what it was like to sleep in a tent and who tactfully brought his own supper with him. After supper, he asked for fireworks (rockets) to be fired, which caused him as much terror as delight.

Such were the first contacts of the French with the natives of this marvellous isle, which Bougainville was soon to call by the suggestive and charming name of La Nouvelle Cythère—the New Cythera.

Chapter Seven

The New Cythera

"Each day", Bougainville says, "the islanders brought us fruits, poultry, pigs, fish and pieces of cloth, when they bartered for nails, tools, beads, buttons and a thousand other trifles which they looked on as treasures." They did everything they could to help the Frenchmen. They helped Commerson to collect remarkable plants and shells of great beauty. They carried wood down to the boats. They were rewarded with nails, for which they seemed to have a particular predeliction.

Yet, as has already been observed from the comments of Commerson, the Tahitians had but the vaguest notions concerning the property of others. "We had always", wrote Bougainville, "to keep a sharp eye on everything we brought ashore, even in our pockets, for Europe has no such adroit pickpockets as the people of this country. Neverthless it did not appear that thieving was one of their habits. Nothing is locked in their houses, everything remains on the ground or is hung up, there are no locks and no guard. Doubtless curiosity for new objects stimulated their cupidity and there are black sheep everywhere. . . ."

The Tahitians stole the most unlikely things. It will be recalled that a pistol was taken from a French officer when Ereti gave his outdoor supper party. Two rifles and a large kettle disappeared from the camp without the knowledge of the sentries, and shirts and pocket handkerchiefs vanished as if by magic. On one occasion, an islander withdrew an officer's sword from his scabbard without his knowledge, while he was admiring the scenery.

Bougainville records how he himself was the victim of an unusual theft. A venerable old man and his three daughters sailed out to the *Boudeuse* by canoe. Bougainville received them in his cabin, and the old man gave him to understand by the most respectful signs that he would be proud and happy if he would accept his three daughters in marriage. Bougainville was obliged, naturally in the most polite manner, to explain to the parent that his obligations would not permit him to accept this generous offer of a conjugal *ménage à quatre*, whereupon the father and his three daughters bade him farewell. No sooner had the visitors left the vessel than Bougainville noticed that his "achromatic glass" (presumably a non-refracting telescope) had disappeared. He at once sent a boat after the canoe, and the old man, guessing that the theft had been discovered, turned to meet the boat and handed the precious glass back to the sailors in the most perfectly natural manner. "This thievish turn of the islanders", continues Bougainville, "affected in no way their friendly relations with us."

Like Commerson, he was inclined to overlook their propensity for stealing.

> Apart from the stealing [he wrote], everything was as pleasant as it could be. Every day our people walked about the country unarmed, alone or in small groups. They were invited into houses and to meals. When, on several occasions, I took walks inland, I could easily have supposed myself transported into the Garden of Eden. We wandered over a grassy plain covered with fine fruit trees, interspersed by little brooks which kept everything beautifully fresh without any of the discomforts of dampness. A large population here enjoys the wealth bestowed upon them by nature. We came upon groups of men and women seated in the shade in the orchards, and they all greeted us in a friendly manner, while those we met on the path stepped aside to let us pass. Everywhere we found hospitality, and leisure, quiet pleasure and all the appearance of happiness.

This idyllic picture was in no way exaggerated. Bougainville goes on to say that the ancients might well have located the Elysian Fields in this landscape, and that the men, many of them over six foot tall, were of splendid appearance.

> Nowhere could a painter have found finer models for a Hercules or a Mars. [As for the women,] their appearance ravished the eye and the heart and all their gestures were harmonious. Nausicaa herself was not endowed with more grace, nor Calypso with a more engaging charm. They were not shy, and it might fairly be said that Venus was their goddess. . . . Here the lot of the women is sweet idleness and the art of pleasing is their most serious occupation. These pleasure-loving habits of the Tahitians give them a noticeably gentle evenness of temper, which is only possible to people who have leisure and are happy. Hence they manifest lightness of character which every day amazes me. . . .

With the exception of rumours of youthful love affairs in London and during his stay in Quebec, we never hear (certainly not from him) of Bougainville having intimate relations with women. Is it possible that a virile man of his character was proof against the seductive beauty of the maidens of Tahiti? Can one believe that Bougainville, who had no objection to his sailors' (and presumably his officers') intimate relations with the dark-eyed and only too willing beauties, did not succumb himself? In fact the Prince of Nassau-Siegen, in his account of the journey, categorically states that Bougainville resisted all temptation.

Bougainville certainly made use of his time in Tahiti to inquire into everything regarding the customs and religion of the islanders.

> Besides a superior being named *Eri-t-Era*, the King of the Sun or Light, a being unrepresented by any material image, the Tahitians acknowledged several divinities, some of whom were benevolent and others malevolent. Without distinguishing one from the other, these divinities are called by the common name of *eatoua*, and they preside over all the acts of life and decide their success or misfortune. In this fair land, human sacrifices are sometimes offered to these deities. [Something Commerson seems to have overlooked.] Anyone who sneezed they saluted with the remark, "*Evarour-t-eatoua* awake you"— or, perhaps, "Let not the evil one put you to sleep." Therein lie traces of common origin with the people of the Old World.

Wishing to provide some permanent expression of his gratitude for the natives' generous and cordial welcome, Bougainville proposed to Ereti (whom he always calls *le bon cacique*) to plant a garden in the French style—an offer which was gratefully accepted. Corn, barley, oats, rice, maize, onions and vegetable seeds were planted. However, the understanding that such acts of friendship promoted between the French and the islanders were very nearly completely destroyed by two regrettable incidents. As the Prince of Nassau-Siegen recounts, "I was walking in the countryside when I suddenly found myself surrounded by men and women in tears who threw themselves into my arms, while others knelt and clutched me round the knees. At first I did not guess the reason for their misery and made it clear to them that we were their friends. 'Alas,' they replied, 'these friends kill us.'"

What had occurred was that on 10 April a native was killed by a shot fired at point-blank range. Despite every effort, Bougainville was unable to find the culprit. To soften the evil effect of the murder, he showered gifts on Ereti, but, just as goodwill was being re-established, three islanders were bayoneted. The murderers were four soldiers who had been haggling over the acquisition of a pig. The other islanders, men, women and children, fled to the mountains. The canoes left the vicinity of the ships. The four soldiers, who were quickly identified, were put in irons awaiting court martial. Ereti showed astonishing forbearance. Obviously terrified that Bougainville would hang the culprits, he carried a palm frond in his hand and, with tears in his eyes, embraced the Prince of Nassau-Siegen, begging that the men should be pardoned. Nevertheless there was an air of insecurity, and, fearing reprisals, Bougainville spent the night on shore with sixty fusiliers to augment the guard round the camp.

Bougainville had already decided to cut short his stay in Tahiti, because of the perilous anchorage of his ships, which were at risk from the reefs with which the bay was strewn. Following the murder, he made preparations to leave immediately. Probably there would have been no reprisals from the natives, who were truly sad to see him leave. It was with every demonstration of lachrymose affection that they bade farewell to their visitors.

The day of departure came. In the evening Bougainville took formal possession of the enchanting island in the name of France. An oak plank on which he had had carved the official act of possession in the name of His Most Christian Majesty was buried near the site of his camp, together with a hermetically sealed bottle containing a parchment inscribed with the names of all the officers who had participated in his journey. As soon as the islanders saw that the ships were making ready to sail, they came in crowds in their canoes to say adieu to the strangers, bringing with them quantities of fruits and other provisions. Ereti went on board the *Boudeuse*, followed by a Tahitian youth named Aotourou, who, although perhaps not so handsome as the other young men of the island, had distinguished himself in his relations with the French by his intelligence and great friendliness. In addition, he had expressed a wish to visit the country of these foreigners. Bougainville had tried to dissuade him, but finally agreed to accept him as a passenger and at the same time promised him the means to return to Tahiti when he wished. Ereti commended Aotourou to Bougainville and all his officers, "saying that this was his friend whom he confided to his friends". After this the Tahitian chief took his leave of the French, embracing each of them in turn, mingling his embraces with tears. In the meanwhile all Ereti's wives, of whom he seemed to have a great number, were on board a canoe alongside the *Boudeuse*, "weeping copiously and lamenting rhythmically", while all the other natives followed their example. "Thus we left these kind people", wrote Bougainville, "and I was no less surprised by the sorrow our departure caused them than I had been by their friendly confidence on our arrival."

Despite the numerous attractions of Tahitian life, Bougainville decided to cut short his stay because of the dangers of the anchorage. Indeed the departure of the two ships (on 15 April, little more than a week after their arrival) was nearly disastrous. The *Boudeuse* was nearly wrecked when weighing anchor, and was saved only by the timely arrival of cutters and longboats, which were able to tow her off as she was being carried away by the tide and a huge wave and was riding dangerously close to the reefs. Bougainville writes in his Journal,

> The worst that shipwreck had so far threatened was that we might have to pass our days on an island endowed with all nature's gifts, and to exchange the delights of our homeland for a peaceable carefree existence. But on this occasion shipwreck was displayed under a more cruel aspect; the ship was being carried rapidly onto the reefs, and would not have stood up to the sea for two minutes; only a few of the

strongest swimmers would have been saved, and then only with difficulty.

As it was, the *Boudeuse* was saved, and she and the *Étoile* resumed their course across the Pacific, while the crew watched with regret the marvellous island of love fade into the clear horizon.

The author's painting of Bougainville's ship *Bondeuse* after her refitting at Brest.

Chapter Eight

Baret's Secret—The Discovery of the Great Cyclades

Commerson stood apart from the others on the deck of the *Étoile*, casting an irritated glance at the shores of Tahiti as they faded into the distance. Only a week before, he had showered blessings on the island as a naturalist's paradise, but now he cursed it for the misadventure that had overtaken his servant Baret and was now so lamentably recoiling on himself. The eminent naturalist felt a blush of shame mounting to his cheeks, which up to now had flushed with excitement only at the discovery of a new botanical or ichthyological discovery. He, Philibert Commerson, one of the most ascetic and virtuous of men, who, before leaving Paris on this expedition had made a will in which he had given the sum of 200 livres for the creation of a prize for virtue, a medal to be awarded each year "to whomsoever should have performed, without motives of ambition, vanity or hypocrisy, the most praiseworthy act of moral or social kind, such for example as a generous sacrifice of his personal interests", he, whose only goddess was science, was now accused of having committed a breach of morals and of having offered up sacrifices to Venus. A sad and perhaps shocking story that is nonetheless worth the telling.

Soon after the *Étoile* had anchored off Tahiti, Aotourou had come on board, and, catching sight of Baret, Commerson's faithful servant, who shared his master's cabin, had showed signs of the most lively interest. There was, however, little in Baret's appearance to arouse so much curiosity. About twenty-six years of age, he was not particularly good looking, just a healthy young fellow with plenty of spirit and an untiring worker. "We had seen him", said Bougainville, "accompanying his master on all his expeditions amidst the snows and icy hills of the Straits of Magellan, carrying, even on those laborious excursions, provisions, arms and portfolios of plants with a courage and strength which gained for him the nickname of Commerson's 'beast of burden'."

Aotourou kept going round and round Baret, constantly repeating the word *aiene*. What could be the meaning of this? Presently came the explanation. In the Tahitian language *aiene* means "girl". Baret's reputation as female spread quickly among the islanders, and on the following day, while he was collecting plants with his master, some of the natives came to pay him admiring homage. One of their number, with the physique of a Hercules, lifted him up like a

E

feather and made off at top speed with his precious burden. By good luck, an officer of Bougainville's staff happened to be nearby, and, drawing his sword, scattered the onlookers and gave chase to the abductor, who was forced to surrender the unfortunate Baret. The crews of the *Boudeuse* and *Étoile* were greatly intrigued by this incident. One of the soldiers determined by hook or by crook to find out the truth, and his indiscreet curiosity revealed to him without a doubt that Aotourou had not been mistaken: Baret was indeed a woman.

The austere naturalist, founder of a prize for virtue, was not spared the jests and teasing of his companions. As for Baret, now Jeanne Baret, she henceforth received solicitous attention from the crew and continued as devoted as ever to Commerson, who in the will that he had made before leaving France had not forgotten to make provision for her.

> She knew from the outset [wrote Bougainville, who, according to Vivès, the surgeon, had long suspected her sex and perhaps had known of it from the start] the goal that was in prospect, and the idea of such a voyage had excited her curiosity. She would be the first woman to accomplish it and I must do her the justice to acknowledge that her behaviour all the time she was on board was a model of propriety. It must be admitted, however, that had the two vessels been shipwrecked in this vast ocean on some desert island, fate would have played some strange tricks on Baret.

Now that her secret was out, it was recollected that she had never changed her underclothes in public and no one could remember ever having seen her shave. She admitted to Bougainville that she was an orphan and had once before acted the part of gentleman's valet, without discovery. It was, however, a boring occupation and she had jumped at the opportunity of entering the service of the great naturalist who had been invited to join Bougainville's expedition.

Aotourou very soon proved a most useful passenger, for he knew every inch of the dangerous waters surrounding Tahiti. Bougainville congratulated himself on having brought with him this warm-hearted and intelligent man, who was not only of inestimable value to the navigators, but also showed a deep attachment to the French commander. Aotourou, as is the custom of his country, exchanged names with Bougainville and, to seal the pact of friendship, wished to be called by his new friend's name. This he pronounced "Boutavéris", which is what he was called henceforth.

On his return to France, Bougainville was criticized, especially by the *philosophes*—Diderot in particular—for having "torn" this young native from his natural surroundings. Bougainville naturally replied that, far from having "torn" the young savage from his native shores, Aotourou had himself begged to accompany him to France.

For a fortnight the *Boudeuse* and the *Étoile* continued their journey without incident. On 3 May the voyagers sighted land to the north-east and, as they drew nearer, observed lights and the smoke of fires and twenty or so figures running along the seashore. Aotourou, who for the occasion discarded the European clothes he had now adopted, was sent ashore, but found that the natives could not understand a word he said. However, the natives, though not hospitable like those of Tahiti, brought the French crew yams, coconuts, water-fowl of superb plumage, fish-hooks and long spears—in exchange for which they would only accept lengths of red flannel. These natives inhabited an archi-pelago named by Bougainville "l'Archipel des Navigateurs"—today known as Samoa. On 22 May, two more islands appeared, the first of which he named, appropriately, Pentecost, and the second of which he called Aurora, as it was first sighted at dawn. A third small isle, shaped like a sugar-loaf, was soon seen on the horizon and was named Étoile Peak.

On the following day they again came in sight of a coastline where it seemed they might conveniently land. Bougainville decided to send three armed boats ashore to collect wood and, if possible, fresh food for the sick, for a large number of the crew and nearly all the officers were again suffering from scurvy. The landing was not accomplished without difficulty. The inhabitants of this country met the French, bow and arrow in hand. The Prince of Nassau-Siegen, however, courageously advanced towards them, and the distribution of gifts of red cloth among them greatly helped to calm their bellicose temper. The sailors were able to cut wood and with great difficulty obtained some fresh fruit from these disagreeable people, who, by way of farewell, launched a hail of arrows on these unwelcome visitors who had intruded on their barbarous solitude. A few musket shots soon put a check on their boldness.

The physique of these natives resembled their character. Bougainville gives a striking description of them:

> These islanders are of two colours, black and mulatto. They have thick lips and woolly hair, which is sometimes yellow. They are small, ugly, malformed and most of them scarred by leprosy, which led to our calling the island Île des Lépreux [Isle of the Lepers]. We saw few women and those we did see were no more pleasing than the men. I noticed that none of the men had beards. . . . Our Tahitian, who had begged to be one of the landing-party, seemed to be as disagreeably impressed by these people as we were. He did not understand a word of their language.

On 26 May, towards the south, an unbroken coastline that appeared to form part of some mainland was sighted. A swarm of very dark-skinned people were running along the beach. Entering a large inlet that seemed to promise suitable anchorage, Bougainville sent several armed boats to reconnoitre. One of the boats, separated from the others, went close inshore, where a couple of arrows discharged in its direction soon revealed the intentions of the natives towards the visitors, who made haste to answer with a volley of musketry. The natives, who seemed to be of the same race as those of the Île des Lépreux, uttered horrible cries and beat frenziedly on a kind of small drum, which emitted most funereal sounds. Bougainville at once ordered the boat to return. "I took steps", he wrote, "to avoid the dishonour of any further abuse of the superiority of our forces."

The hostility of the natives made all idea of landing impossible, but the reconnaissance carried out by the boats from the *Boudeuse* proved, from a geographical point of view, useful, for what had at first been taken for an unbroken coastline proved to be, as Bougainville records, "no more than a string of islands, one overlapping the other, and . . . the bay was a meeting place of the several channels that separated them."

Bougainville named the islands (now known as the New Hebrides) the Archipelago of the Great Cyclades. It was this same archipelago that the Portuguese navigator Fernandes de Queiros had sighted in 1606, had mistaken for a continent, and had named Espiritu Santo. Bougainville had just unmasked an error which had persisted for a century and a half; but he wished to prove once and for all that the famous continent consisted of no more than an agglomeration of islands.

Most geographers had maintained that Espiritu Santo and New Guinea formed part of one and the same continent. To disprove them it was necessary for Bougainville to continue westward for approximately a further thousand miles, but, as provisions were becoming scarce and there was no certainty that the French explorers would be able to replenish their stores during such a lengthy détour, the wisest course was to make for some European settlement. However, as Maurice Thiéry states, "Wisdom is not a characteristic of great navigators, and what mattered famine or danger when it lay within their power to add by this new discovery to the sum of the world's knowledge?"

Chapter Nine

New Discoveries—New Britain

Bougainville continued his westerly course for twelve days. On 10 June land was sighted, which he called New Holland. This was in fact Australia. "I have seen few countries", he wrote, "which at first sight appeared so beautiful. A flat country divided into plains and groves ran along the shore and then rose like an amphitheatre to mountains whose summits were lost in the clouds. The sad state to which we were reduced gave us no time to visit this magnificent country, so rich in promise of wealth and fertility."

Having proved what he had set out to prove—that the "southern land of Santo Spiritu was unattached to any continent" Bougainville decided to turn north-east. Apart from sighting one island (Ushant), he saw nothing more until 25 June, when high land terminating in a cape, which Bougainville called Cape Deliverance, came into sight. "It is land", he said, "which we have justly acquired the right to name (since no European has hitherto sighted it) Louisiade." He was thus rewarded for his endurance and the dangers which he and his companions had faced when they had put out into the unknown. Certainly the hardships and dangers that he and his crew had endured were very great. Since leaving Tahiti, no stores worth mentioning had been obtainable and their provisions were rapidly diminishing. The salt meat had gone bad and there was a lack of drinking water. Even rats had come to be regarded as a delicacy by sailors reduced to chewing leather. Hunger brought on a recurrence of scurvy. Bougainville made every effort to comfort the sick. He kept remarkably cool and managed the navigation, often in storm and mist, with consummate skill. He remained remarkably fit in the circumstances. He was, as we know, always fresh complexioned and on the plump side, which prompted the young St-Germain to suggest that he had his own secret store of provisions which he shared with the aristocratic members of his staff. Even if he did reserve some fresh fruit for himself (of which there is no proof, though it is known that he drank lemonade and chocolate) he can hardly be condemned, for, if the commander had fallen sick, the whole expedition would inevitably have foundered. None of his officers received extra rations.

On 30 June a mountainous island was sighted from which a dozen canoes put out, containing "savages as black as African negroes, armed with arrows

and spears, whose intentions did not appear entirely pacific". Boats sent out to
explore the coasts returned to report that a landing there was out of the question.
The next day the *Étoile* and *Boudeuse* ran along the coast in such torrential rain
that it was impossible to see anything clearly. At last an attractive-looking bay
was observed and Bougainville sent out boats to make the necessary soundings.
During these operations, ten canoes appeared.

> In these craft [wrote Bougainville] were some 150 men armed with
> bows, spears and shields. These canoes advanced in good order, being
> paddled towards our ships, and when they judged themselves to be
> close enough, they very slowly separated in order to surround us.
> The Indians uttered piercing cries, and seizing their bows and spears
> began an attack, which they thought no doubt would be child's play
> against a mere handful of men. A first volley of musketry did not check
> them, and they continued to discharge their arrows and javelins,
> covering themselves with their shields. . . . A second volley, however,
> put them to flight, many flinging themselves into the water to swim
> ashore. Two of their canoes were captured. They were very long and
> well constructed. At the prow of one of them was carved a man's head,
> with eyes of mother-of-pearl, ears of tortoiseshell, and the face, which
> resembled a mask, decorated with a long beard, the lips being painted
> a brilliant red. Inside their canoes was found a great quantity of bows
> and arrows, spears and shields; coconuts and different fruits, of what
> species we knew not; various little articles made use of by these
> Indians; very fine nets neatly woven; and the half-grilled jawbone of
> a man. The islanders are black, with curly hair which they dye white,
> yellow or red. Their audacity in attacking us, the habit of carrying
> offensive and defensive weapons, and the skill in making use of them,
> proved to us that they are accustomed to fighting. . . . We called the
> river and creek from which these brave islanders issued, "La Rivière
> des Guerriers" [Warriors' River], and the whole island and bay,
> Choiseul.

As the wind had dropped and the tide was contrary, any idea of anchorage in
Choiseul Bay had to be abandoned, and they continued their course, cruising
along part of a fairly large island separated from Choiseul Island by a wide
channel. Both the island and the channel the crews named after their commander,
in affectionate admiration, so immortalizing his name upon the map of the
Pacific.

Many other islands were sighted, but either the natives proved so extremely
hostile that a landing was impossible, or the islands provided no fruit or vegetables for the now scurvy-ridden crew.

On 5 July an apparently immense island came into view, and a magnificent bay was seen. Bougainville immediately gave the order to drop anchors. The island appeared to be uninhabited, but, again, no fruit or vegetables could be found, even the fishing was bad, and there was practically no game. However, the ships were able to take on supplies of wood and fresh water, and certain species of insects delighted Commerson, who wrote minute descriptions of them and preserved them for future generations of entomologists. One day a sailor digging for shells made a remarkable discovery, for, by an unbelievable coincidence, he found buried in the sand a portion of a leaden plate on which the remains of a few words in English were written. Bougainville learned later that this plate had been deposited by Philip Carteret, who had put into the same bay with the *Swallow* in the previous year. (The *Swallow* had originally sailed with Wallis's *Dolphin*, but had become separated from it in the Straits of Magellan and thence had proceeded alone.) "It was a singular chance", Bougainville wrote, "that of all the many islands, we should have been led to the very same spot where a rival nation had left a memorial of an undertaking similar to our own."

Bougainville rightly guessed that the island was none other than New Britain and that the place where he was now anchored (which he called Port Praslin, after Louis XV's Minister of Marine) was part of the vast bay of St George that the English navigator William Dampier had entered in 1700. Dampier had had the good fortune to light on an uninhabited district, which, as Bougainville puts it, "provided him with rest, and whose products caused him to conceive great hopes concerning this country . . . while we landed in the middle of a desert which only yielded us water and wood". Desert it might have been, but Bougainville waxes lyrical over the beauties of the landscape, "worthy of the brush of the greatest painters". Considering that his crew was almost starving and that the weather was atrocious, with constant torrential rains, thunderstorms and gale-force winds, it is remarkable that he could still feel an interest in the beauties of nature.

For a fortnight more they coasted along the southern shores of New Britain. The island, as they soon found, was by no means uninhabited. From time to time canoes, manned by hideous natives, put out from the shore and surrounded the ships, "showing", as Bougainville relates, "their treacherous and bellicose intentions beyond any doubt. A few musket shots would send them flying, but there could be, of course, no question of obtaining fresh provisions from them or any kind of trading."

The question of the food supply of the ships became daily more serious.

> I was once more forced [wrote Bougainville] to take an ounce off the bread ration. The small remaining supplies were in part spoiled; at any other time the salt provisions would have been thrown overboard, but the bad had to be eaten along with the good. Who could foretell when this state of affairs would end? Such was our fate, to suffer at one and

the same time from the past, which had weakened us, and from the present, whose recurrent tragedy was the awful uncertainty as to how long this state of affairs was to last. This was our worst trouble and my distress was multiplied by that of others. I must nevertheless put it on record that not one among them gave way to despair. . . . The officers set the example, and not a single night did the sailors miss their dancing, whether food was scanty or abundant. It had never been necessary to double their pay.

British sailors were by no means the only seamen to enjoy hornpipes, sea shanties and dancing.

Chapter Ten

Relief at Last—The Moluccas

It was not until 26 August that the crews' hopes of relief were realized. At last they were entering the Molucca Straits, where the Dutch had rich colonial settlements. Four days later an extensive island was sighted which proved to be Ceram, one of the many islands of the Molucca archipelago. Two days later Bougainville was at the entrance to a bay of this island. He had the Dutch flag and pennant hoisted and fired a salute of cannon. "I made an error without being aware of it," Bougainville wrote later, "for we learned afterwards that the inhabitants of Ceram were at war with the Dutch, whom they have driven from almost every part of their island. So it was in vain that we put in; the boats took refuge in shore, and we profited by a fresh breeze to continue our course.'

This must have been a disappointment indeed to the starving and sick crews, but at six o'clock in the evening of that same day they saw two fires burning on land. Bougainville did not doubt for a moment that this was the island of Burou, where the Dutch East India Company had an important settlement. "The first gleam of sunlight showed that we had not been mistaken", he wrote. He goes on to describe the heartfelt enthusiasm felt by all the crew at the sight of the port of Cajeli,

> which to the dazzled eyes of the sailors appeared like a corner of Paradise transplanted thither by some fantastic upheaval of nature. It was not without extreme delight that at daybreak we discovered the entry to the Bay of Cajeli (where the Dutch have their settlement), for here our misery came to an end. Scurvy had made cruel ravages among us since we left Port Praslin; no one was altogether free from it, and half of our crew were unfit for duty. Our remaining stores were quite putrid and smelt so rank that for some time past the worst moments of our sad days had been those when the bell rang for meals; and how amazingly did the contrast of our present condition enrich the charms of the Burou coast in our eyes. From midnight onwards, from miles out at sea, an agreeable perfume exhaled by the aromatic plants with which the Molucca Islands are covered had been noticed and it seemed to herald the end of our misfortunes. The view of a

fairly large town, situated at the end of a gulf, where we anchored, and the sight of cattle wandering in the meadows which surround the town caused transports of delight, which, though I most certainly shared in them, I find impossible to describe.

No sooner had the vessels dropped anchor than two Dutch soldiers came aboard the *Boudeuse*. These were the first Europeans on whom the navigators had set eyes since they had left Montevideo. One of these soldiers, who spoke French, inquired on behalf of the Resident of the Dutch factory what special grounds Bougainville had for calling at this port, which was reserved for ships of the Dutch East India Company.

"I sent them back", writes Bougainville, "with an officer . . . to report that only necessity of getting provisions had forced us to enter the first port we came to, and that we should leave immediately the Resident had supplied us with the help of which we were in the most extreme need. We could not stop to consider treaties forbidding foreign vessels to put into the port of Molucca."

The soldiers returned shortly with a message from the Resident inviting Bougainville to send him a written declaration of his reasons, so that he could justify himself to his superiors. Naturally Bougainville was only too pleased to acquiesce, and henceforth all difficulties were surmounted. Heinriks Ouman, the Resident, accorded the French a most cordial welcome and at once invited the officers of the two ships to supper. This first civilized meal for many a month left an ineffaceable impression on the minds of the famished Frenchmen. Bougainville wrote later,

> The eagerness and the enjoyment with which we devoured this supper proved better than any words we could have spoken our need, and that it was not without reason that we claimed to be short of food. All the Dutch were in ecstasies and they almost feared to eat anything at all, lest they should be depriving us. One has to be a sailor and to have been reduced to the extremities we had endured for several months to form any idea of the sensation produced in people reduced to such a state by the sight of salads and other components of a good supper. This supper was for me one of the most delicious incidents of my whole life, and all the more so because I had been able to put aboard the vessels enough for everybody to sup as well as we were doing, and in the same style as ourselves.

The six days spent on this delightful island were days of consolation and enchantment. The sick, who had at once been sent ashore, immediately responded to better food and treatment. Soldiers and sailors amused themselves like children, scampering about the woods regardless of the serpents, but enchanted by the multicoloured parakeets and other birds which fluttered and chattered in the treetops. One sailor was bitten on the ear by a venomous snake, but was soon cured by the ships' doctors, while Aoutourou looked on amazed. In Tahiti a snake bite was considered inevitably lethal.

Bougainville, no less, was overcome by the charms of the landscape, "intersected by groves, plains and hillsides and with valleys watered by delightful streams". He several times took part in deer hunts, "for in the island that graceful creature is to be found in large numbers".

The Resident kept open house for the French. As Bougainville says,

> His house was ours, and at any hour of the day food and drink were at hand, a form of politeness which was much appreciated, especially for men who were still suffering from the effects of famine. He held two formal banquets in our honour, at which the cleanliness, elegance and excellent fare to be found in such an out-of-the-way place really surprised us. The home of this worthy Dutchman is charming, elegantly furnished entirely *à la chinoise*. Everything is arranged for coolness; it is surrounded by gardens through which flows a river; the approach to the seashore is by an avenue of large trees. His wife and daughters, dressed in Chinese costumes, perform the honours of the house most charmingly. They spend their time preparing flowers for distillation, tying up bouquets and preparing betel nuts. The air breathed in this agreeable house is deliciously perfumed and all of us would have most willingly lingered there.

Aotourou fell from ecstasy into ecstasy at the sight of objects and customs so unfamiliar to him, and did his best to imitate his French friends at table, on visits, or when out walking. His greatest desire was to appear highly civilized; he told the Dutch that he was a chief in his own country and was travelling for his pleasure with his friends. From time to time he would ask Bougainville if Paris were as beautiful as Cajeli.

The days slipped by with disconcerting rapidity in this land of delight, but to remain longer was out of the question. Advantage had to be taken of favourable winds to sail for Batavia (Djakarta), where Bougainville had decided to stop for a long time for repairs and refitting. He bought eighteen oxen and a quantity of sheep and poultry to provide sufficient fresh food for the journey there.

Bougainville received a shock when the worthy Resident presented him with the bill: the price of livestock had risen to colossal proportions. It was obvious that Mijnheer Ouman, worthy employee of the Dutch East India Company that he was, had made a good profit for his masters and had certainly not forgotten himself.

On 7 September the ships set sail and the voyagers "bade farewell to the perfumed isle on whose flowery shores they had recovered joy and health".

Chapter Eleven

Homecoming

To discourage foreign ships from using the Straits of Molucca, which the Dutch regarded as their own property, they represented the navigation of them as extremely dangerous. Bougainville fully appreciated, however, that, perilou- and dangerous as the straits might be, they were far less hazardous than seas through which he had already sailed. He had no hesitation, therefore, in direcs ting his course towards the Straits of Butung, a passage formed by an arm of the sea between Celebes and Butung Island. The eastern coast of Celebes particularly delighted the eyes of the navigators, "by the variety of its plains, its hillsides and its mountains, where luxuriant verdure displayed all manner of dazzling colours", wrote Commerson.

Canoes now frequently came alongside the *Boudeuse* and *Étoile*, and the Malay natives brought fowls, eggs and bananas for sale, also parakeets and cockatoos. "All these people", wrote Commerson, "are small, ugly and very swarthy. Their religion is that of Mahomet. They appeared to be shrewd traders, but are gentle and keep faith."

On 15 September, a Malay pilot was engaged to take them through the Straits of Butung. "He did his work conscientiously and the straits were passed without incident", reports Bougainville. "An abundance of canoes was con- stantly about, the ships coming and going as at a fair, laden with refreshments, curios and pieces of cloth. The ships, now overflowing with provisions, decks and yard-arms swarming with clacking poultry, brought to mind a market day in a country town."

An old man, probably the father of the pilot, came on board the *Boudeuse*. Like his son, he refused all food offered him and contented himself with bananas and chewing betel nuts. Father and son, both devout Muslims, were, however, less abstemious where drink was concerned. They drank, Bougainville tells us, large quantities of brandy—assuring themselves, no doubt, that it was only the drinking of wine that Mahomet had forbidden. Five *oracaies*, or chiefs, from Butung also visited the ship, saying that they had come to pay their respects to the representatives of the Dutch East India company.

When they were informed [says Bougainville] that we were French, they were by no means put out, and offered their respects to France.

Their welcome aboard was accompanied by the gift of a roebuck. I gave them, in the name of the King, a present of some silk materials, which they divided into five lots, and I taught them to recognize the French flag. I offered them some brandy, which is obviously what they were expecting, and it seems that, like the pilot and his father, they were allowed by Mahomet to drink to the prosperity of the sovereigns of Butung and of France, and to that of the Dutch East India Company and our journey, so long as they did not do so with wine. They then offered me all the assistance in their power, adding that at different times during the last three years three English vessels had passed this way, to whom they had supplied water, wood, poultry and fruit, saying that they were their friends and that they were sure that we too would be theirs. They had by now already drunk several bumpers . . . after this speech their glasses were replenished. Having taken their leave of us, the *oracaies* next paid a visit to the *Étoile*, where they drank to the health of their second group of newfound friends; and, when the time came for them to leave, they had to be lent a supporting hand to embark them in their canoes.

On 28 September the navigators entered the magnificent bay of Batavia, where they were to enjoy all the refinements of civilization. "After having been at sea", wrote Bougainville, "for eighteen and a half months since leaving Montevideo . . . we arrived at one of the most beautiful colonies in the world, which we all regarded as the end of our voyage."

The necessary permits having been received, the ships were handed over to be refitted. The sick were sent ashore and comfortably installed in the hospital. All necessary proceedings relating to provisions and supplies for the ships were concluded with the senior officials of the Dutch East India Company. All Dutchmen resident in Batavia were officials of the company, which seemed to behave generously towards its employees, since they all appeared to live in splendid opulence, from which Bougainville inferred that personal profits, not always admissible, might very likely be added to the official salaries received by these zealous employees.

The French received the most cordial and friendly welcomes from all the high-ranking officials to whom they paid their respects. The all-powerful Governor-General, van der Para, offered them any assistance of which they might stand in need. Bougainville and his companions were constantly invited to dinners in town and in the country, to concerts, to charming excursions and to plays.

We never grew tired [he wrote] of visiting the charming country and people of Batavia. All Europeans, even those accustomed to the finest capitals, would be astonished at the splendour of this city, which is full

of magnificent houses surrounded by superb gardens, kept up with
that taste and cleanliness which has so struck us in all Dutch countries.
I should not be afraid to assert that they surpass in beauty and richness
those of our largest towns in France, and that they even approach the
magnificence of the outskirts of Paris.

But what most caught Bougainville's observant eye was the sight "of numerous
peoples, who although entirely different from each other in morals, customs,
religions and race, yet form a single united society . . . (Dutch, Chinese, Malays
and negroes)".

The streets were fine and spacious and the canals bordered by trees increased
the charm of the town, though unfortunately the canals were breeding grounds
for mosquitoes and the sanitary conditions of this fine town were deplorable.
Malaria and dysentery were endemic, and both officers and men suffered,
especially from the latter. Aotourou, too, fell a victim to dysentry, and henceforth called Batavia *enoua maté*—" the land that kills". As the scurvy patients
showed no signs of recovering completely, Bougainville, thinking that a pro-
longed stay in Batavia might cause even greater ravages among his men than
the whole of his long voyage, began to hasten his preparations for departure.

On 17 October, the *Boudeuse* and *Étoile* left the beautiful but unhealthy
harbour. Their next objective was Île-de-France, today known as Mauritius.
The weather was superb and the winds so favourable that it took them no more
than three weeks to arrive at their destination. Bougainville describes his profound emotion at the sight of the white flag of France with its fleurs-de-lis
flying over the harbour of this little corner of the motherland. However, the
joy of finding themselves once more on French soil was overshadowed by the
death of the Chevalier de Bouchage, who died from the after-effects of dysentery
contracted in Batavia. Bougainville said of him, "He was a man of distinguished
merit, who, added to the knowledge which goes to make a great sea officer,
possessed all the qualities of heart and mind which render a man dear in the
eyes of his friends."

A few days later after the loss of this excellent officer, they had to mourn
the death of a young volunteer who for some time had been suffering from a
chest complaint. At their own request, Bougainville left behind in Mauritius
twenty-three soldiers, several pilot-apprentices, an engineer (presumably the
one he had picked up in the Falkland Islands) and Veron, the astronomer. St-
Germain, the writer to the *Boudeuse*, who had been seriously ill with scurvy, was
also landed on the island, where he soon recovered his health. Commerson, who,
despite the peaceful voyage from Batavia, had once again suffered from acute
seasickness, was only too happy to set foot on French territory, and expressed
to Bougainville his intention of remaining on the island to examine its natural
history and that of Madagascar. His faithful Jeanne Baret refused to leave him
(since leaving Tahiti, they had on Bougainville's orders had to occupy separate

sleeping quarters), and "continued to lavish her care upon him with touching devotion". He died five years later, after making some interesting observations in Madagascar, including a description of a tribe of autochthonous pygmies, the Quismos, who are now extinct, and listing many new plants. Jeanne was with him when he died. It is said that after the death of her master she entered into lawful wedlock with a soldier stationed on Mauritius and later returned to Europe. No more is known of her, but Commerson had provided for her in his will, and it is to be hoped that she lived "happily ever after".

Bougainville left Mauritius on 12 December; the *Étoile*, whose repairs were not yet completed, left a month later, losing two men *en route* through sickness. The return journey took three months and passed without incident. It was rendered all the more agreeable by a fortnight's stop at the Cape, where the Dutch officials extended their customary warm welcome to Bougainville and his crew. He also met a colony of Huguenots from Rochelle who had settled there after the revocation of the edict of Nantes; they too gave the crew a hospitable welcome. Another, shorter stop was made at Ascension Island, where the crew captured seventy large turtles, for already the ship was running out of fresh food. On approaching the coast of Europe the *Boudeuse* overhauled Captain Carteret's *Swallow*, which had been ahead of her at New Britain. Bougainville recorded,

> I offered to do anything for M. Carteret that might be possible at sea. Carteret replied that he was in need of nothing, but on informing me that he had been handed letters for France at the Cape, I sent on board his ship to fetch them. He made me a present of an arrow which he had picked up on one of the islands he had discovered on his journey round the world—a voyage that he was far from suspecting we had also accomplished. His ship was very small and sailed very badly. What sufferings he must have endured in such an unseaworthy craft.

It had been Bougainville's intention to enter the harbour of Brest, but the bad condition of his masts, which would not have stood up against the equinoctial gales that were then raging in the seas near the port, decided him to put in at St Malo instead. "I entered the harbour", he wrote, "on 16 March 1769, after midday, having lost only seven men in the two years and four months which had elapsed since leaving Nantes."

The young Prince of Nassau-Siegen was the first to praise publicly the great navigator: "Sorti de la carrière d'un militaire de terre dans laquelle il a su se distinguer, il venait d'exécuter heureusement le plus grand ouvrage d'un marin" ["After quitting a distinguished military career on land, he has just happily achieved the greatest feat accomplished by any sailor"]. As Bougainville's biographer Maurice Thiéry writes,

France had every right to be proud of the intrepid navigator, who, admirably seconded by men worthy of their chief, had enriched her colonial and scientific domain by considerable discoveries, and who had been the first among her sons to carry round the world the white flag of their beloved country.

BOOK THREE

AGE AND HONOURS

Bournaria, discovered by Commerson on Reunion
Island. It belongs to the family of Ericaceae.

Bernadesia discovered by Commerson in Tierra del Fuega.

Chapter One

Author and Post Captain

Bougainville was greeted in Paris and at Court as a hero, but his happiness was marred by the fact that his benefactor and friend d'Arboulin was dead, as was his beloved *maman*, Mme Hérault. Since her son, his greatest friend, had been killed at the Battle of Minden, and his dear brother had died six years previously, he had few old friends left with whom to share his experiences. His old patron Madame de Pompadour had also died, without any great sign of regret on the part of the King, and had been supplanted "by a flower, picked from the gutter", Jeanne Bécu, who by means of a dishonourable and dishonouring marriage had become the Comtesse du Barry. She was now *maîtresse en titre* and continued to be the King's favourite until his death.

After a very brief period of rest, Bougainville once more set to work. He began to catalogue the maps and charts that he and his associates had made during his voyage, as well as the nautical and astronomical observations that had been taken. As soon as he had completed his first technical report, he decided to write an account of his adventurous journey for the general public. In 1771, two and a half years after his return, he published *Le Voyage de Bougainville* in two volumes. To have completed his technical report and written his book in such a short space of time seems almost incredible. As René de Kérallain writes,

> The clearness of style, the writer's entire sincerity, the striking simplicity of the narrative and the vivacious descriptions of his adventures, were qualities which assured the work an overwhelming success, at which Bougainville was the only man to be surprised. Modest, like all true heroes, he apologizes in his preface for the literary poverty of his work: "I live far away from the shrines of knowledge and literature, and my ideas and my style still bear the stamp of the wild and roaming life I have led for the last twelve years. It is neither in the great forests of Canada nor upon the bosom of the ocean that one acquires literary art: moreover I have lost that brother whose writings were beloved by the public, and had he still been living, would have come to my aid."

Unselfish as always, he concludes his account of his long and perilous journey, "I must finish this recital by rendering justice to the fine courage, the zeal and invincible patience of the officers and crews of my two vessels. Their constancy stood the proof even in the most trying circumstances, and their goodwill never failed for an instant. . . ."

Even Diderot, although disapproving of Bougainville's "corruption" of natives, wrote of his work that it was "sans apprêt, le ton de la chose, de la simplicité et de la clarté" ["the style of his expression is without pretension, simple and clear"].

Thus, except by a few carping critics, his work was universally acclaimed. To these carping critics Bougainville answered scornfully, "I am a traveller and sailor, that is to say a liar and an imbecile in the eyes of those idle and high and mighty writers, who, confined to their sombre studies, philosophize interminably on the world and its inhabitants and pontificate on nature as they imagine it." He considered that he had not written "a work for entertainment, and that only mariners would benefit from it; and that society was only interested in journeys made in time of war". But he was wrong: there is no doubt that the King and "society" found his adventures most entertaining.

Aotourou, who had accompanied Bougainville to Versailles, caused a great sensation. The Duchesse de Choiseul took him under her special protection and lavished presents on him. Bougainville said of him, "He never failed to notice those who had been kind to him, nor were they ever forgotten in his grateful heart. He was particularly attached to Mme la Duchesse de Choiseul, who had done a great deal for him and shown him special marks of interest and friendship, by which he seemed more touched than by her presents."

Aotourou liked to roam around alone and make his purchases without the help of anyone else. No one, we are told, tried to take advantage of his ignorance of money values and scarcely ever did he pay more than things were worth. His great joy was to visit the Opéra, for he was passionately fond of dancing, though no doubt he thought the ballerinas ridiculously overdressed compared with the dusky beauties of his native land.

The first time that he visited the Royal Gardens (Jardin des Plantes) he saw a tree similar to one that grew in the forests of Tahiti. He rushed towards it and, casting his arms around its trunk, burst into tears. This incident was widely publicized and afforded fuel for the *philosophes'* attacks on Bougainville for having "torn away this simple savage from his native shores". It also provided the poet Delille with inspiration for a poem. It is true that, after eleven blissful months, Aotourou had become homesick, and he expressed a wish to return home. Faithful to his promise, Bougainville took the necessary steps for the repatriation of his protégé. In March 1770 Aotourou embarked on the *Brisson*, which landed him on Mauritius. The Governor of the little colony had received orders from the Ministry of Marine to send the young Tahitian on to his native island. Bougainville devoted 36,000 francs, a third of his estate, to the equipment of the ship that was to perform this journey. In August 1771 the ship, with Aotourou on board, set course for Tahiti. But Aotourou was never to see his home again and there recount to his people his marvellous experiences. An epidemic of smallpox broke out in the ship, and poor Aotourou was one of the first to die.

Bougainville, having finished his book, was not a man to remain inactive. His circumnavigation of the world had by no means satisfied his taste for adventure. Like others before him, he conceived the idea of finding a north-west passage through Arctic waters. Having assured himself of the co-operation of the famous geographer Cassini, he prepared plans for this bold expedition, in the hope of getting it subsidized by the Ministry of Marine. His personal means were insufficient to cover the whole cost. His journey round the world had already involved him in debt. 50,000 francs were owing to him by the State on account of "wages, board and advances made to the crews", but this money had never been paid; only a small annuity had been granted him.

Bougainville, once all his plans were completed, applied to the Minister of Marine, Bourgeois de Boynes, for a subsidy, but was told that no funds were available for polar exploration. The tone of the Minister's refusal implied that Bougainville was asking for public funds in the hopes of procuring a sinecure for himself. Extremely offended, Bougainville is said to have retorted sharply, "Do you imagine, Monsieur, that I should have an easy time of it . . . high pay . . . and hardly any work to do, as though I were asking for a prebend?" Like so many famous sayings, this reply, which is also attributed to the polar explorer Jean Charcot (1867–1936), may well be apocryphal. (The riposte "At least you don't speak like a horse" has also been attributed to men other than Bougainville.)

For lack of funds, therefore, the polar expedition was not to be realized. The Royal Society of London, however, informed of the obstacles put in the way of their distinguished member, invited him to send a memorandum on his proposed expedition. Bougainville generously complied. The English captain Phipps (later Lord Mulgrave, who discovered the Marshall Islands) made use of the plans drawn up by the French navigator, but Phipps's expedition was only half successful, since, of the two possible routes indicated by Bougainville, he chose the one that his French colleague thought the less suitable.

The era of great voyages had closed for Bougainville, but he did not altogether abandon the sea. In 1775 and the two following years, he took part as a post captain in squadron manoeuvres under the command of such distinguished admirals as Luc-Urbain de Guichen, the Comte de Chaffault and the Comte de La Motte-Picquet. Under such chiefs he learned much of naval strategy—an opinion not shared by many regular aristocratic naval officers, who, although with far less experience than Bougainville, regarded this ex-colonel as a mere amateur. Bougainville was never to forget the fact that it was aristocratic birth, far more than experience, that led to promotion. We are on the eve of the French Revolution, and Bougainville, the most loyal of the King's subjects, was actually accused of fomenting revolutionary ideas—but of this later.

Chapter Two

The Comte d'Estaing's Squadron

On 4 July 1776, the thirteen rebel colonies of British North America proclaimed their independence. The news was greeted with enthusiasm in France, where many rejoiced at the thought that the Treaty of Paris was about to be avenged. At the outbreak of Anglo-American hostilities, as all the world knows, the young Marquis de La Fayette, scarcely thirty years of age, had gone to America, in a frigate purchased at his own expense, to place his sword at the service of the insurgents. An extraordinary wave of sympathy for the colonists swept through the ranks of the French nobility. This phenomenon, which cannot be attributed entirely to a hatred of the British, is not easily explained. Volunteers bearing some of the noblest names in France followed La Fayette's example—the Comte de Rochambeau, the Duc de Lauzan, the Duc de Noailles, the Comte de Ségui, the Marquis de la Rouerie, the Vicomte de Maurois, and others. This influx of French noblemen was not always welcome to Washington, for most expected to be given military rank commensurate with their titles. Many, in fact, proved more of an embarrassment than a help. La Fayette and Rochambeau were exceptions, as was the quixotic La Rouerie, who, after meeting with a cold welcome, borrowed sufficient money to raise a troop of irregular sharp-shooters and was finally given a commission and fought brilliantly.

When Benjamin Franklin arrived in Paris to negotiate a Franco-American alliance with M. de Vergennes, Louis XVI's Minister of Foreign Affairs, he received a hero's welcome. "With his long unpowdered hair and his sombre unornamented costume, he represented for France all the noble simplicity of a young nation." On 17 December 1777, Franklin was advised that France had decided to recognize the independence of the United States and to sign a treaty of friendship and of commerce with the Americans. On 6 February 1778, this treaty was finally accepted by both countries and the Anglo-American war became an Anglo-French war, which soon became an Anglo-European one. Vergennes first concluded an alliance with Spain and Holland and then exploited the resentment that all maritime powers felt at Britain's arrogation to herself of a right to search all vessels, regardless of nationality, in case they were carrying contraband of war. Through the intervention of the Empress Catherine of Russia, Vergennes succeeded in grouping Denmark, Prussia, Sweden and Portugal into a league of armed neutrality.

Britain was isolated and the French fleet reorganized by Choiseul after the Treaty of Paris was ready to take its revenge on the old enemy who had so long humiliated it.

In 1778 the Comte de Sartine, Minister of Marine, organized a squadron of twelve warships at Toulon. Command of it was given to Vice-Admiral the Comte d'Estaing, who was given orders to go to the help of the American insurgents and, should circumstances permit, recapture the islands in the West Indies that the British had taken from the French at the time of the Seven Years War.

On 15 March, Bougainville, who was in Brest at the time received orders to report to Toulon without delay to take command of an old battleship named *Le Guerrier*, which belonged to d'Estaing's squadron. On 13 April the little fleet set sail for North America. From letters and diaries written by Bougainville while on board and assiduously collected by René de Kérallain, it is clear that he was far from happy with his new command. He was not particularly pleased with the old vessel given into his charge, or with the crew, none of whom he knew. Most of them were natives of Provence and understood little or no French. After a few days at sea, Bougainville wrote, "Since our departure, I have been tired out, being on deck day and night without other help than that of the boatswain, who, excellent fellow though he is, has, like myself, been half killed with work." What of his fellow officers? He makes no mention of them. The supply work had been inefficiently carried out and Bougainville strongly criticized those responsible. His first thought had always been for the welfare of men under his command. He strongly castigated those noble officers who neglected the well-being of the ordinary seamen and in an angry moment wrote,

> The greatest of our evils, which cannot ever be realized by those happy men who have never left shore, is that for the last five days we have been unable to open either the large or small ports between decks. The atmosphere is foul. Healthy men breathe the same poisonous air as the sick, who are thrown out of their bunks and buffeted by rolling seas, wallow in water and their own excrement and are constantly in a condition worse than death itself. All help, every means which humanity can invent, are powerless against the seas lashed to fury by the winds at this season of the year. Oh that a humanitarian captain, a friend of man, would propose that the large main stern cabin of a man o' war, used by the captain, should be used as a hospital and that the Navy Board, which unanimously refuses such an angelic proposal, should be condemned to spend two years shut up between decks in a vessel rolling in seas off the Newfoundland banks.

On 8 July, after a stormy passage, d'Estaing's squadron arrived in Delaware Bay—too late to engage the British squadron, which had sought safety in the harbour of New York. Bougainville had never had much confidence in the Americans and what he now learned only confirmed his first impressions. He had never forgotten the differences which had existed between the colonial states during his service in Canada. "In this country", he wrote, "there are powerful cabals and the great Washington is himself constantly obliged to contend with them. It is he alone who upholds America and seeks to free her from the fetters of the mother country."

It was at about this time that Bougainville was obliged to order the arrest of the *Guerrier*'s chaplain, "the most detestable of the entire species that could be found among the whole papal militia". This chaplain had a pronounced taste for drink and "for the fleeting pleasures of this world", and, as he appeared to be "more a servant of the Devil than of the Lord", Bougainville, who, though not a particularly religious man himself, had always been careful that religious things should be respected, now assumed episcopal authority and forbade him to say mass. This eccentric priest was later defrocked by a council of chaplains assembled in Boston.

Despite unpleasant incidents such as this and the abominable passage in the old vessel, his Provençal crew had grown to appreciate the true calibre of their commander, whose first regard was always for his men. Then, on 21 August, the Marquis de La Fayette came aboard to present Bougainville with the sword of his old friend and former commander, Montcalm, "With tears in my eyes I kissed it," wrote the General's former aide-de-camp, "and it even became more precious to me for the sake of the young and valiant knight at whose hands I received it." But Bougainville was far from content. Like Nelson some sixty years later, he demanded action at all costs. As day after day passed and d'Estaing still hesitated to seek out the British fleet, so Bougainville's temper rose. It was true that d'Estaing's squadron had been delayed by storm, and his ships needed repair, but the Vice-Admiral's pusillanimous behaviour in coming to a decision to attack Newport, then occupied by the British, drove Bougainville and the Americans to fury.

> In God's name [he exclaimed], let us decide and then act, and when once we have secured the safety of the squadron, the men will at least enjoy the rest they have deserved. I observe, with profound sorrow, that it is always usual at councils and discussions to pay no heed whatsoever to the physical condition of our soldiers and sailors, as if their health was not the basis of all operations. It needs also to be remembered that their morale is considerably affected by this cause, especially when they have to blame the negligence of their commanding officers for their physical sufferings.

The Americans showed no love for their French allies. They not only forgot that it was storms that had prevented d'Estaing from arriving in time to bring support to their forces before Newport, but also blamed d'Estaing for the delays

in refitting his ships. In fact, such was the animosity shown by the citizens of
Boston to the French that shore-leave for the long-suffering crews of d'Estaing's
squadron had to be cancelled. Even though in "friendly" waters, they had to
endure a scarcity of fresh water and lack of fresh provisions, and were subject to
sickness, scurvy and every kind of hardship. Had shore-leave been granted,
many of the already undermanned crews would undoubtedly have deserted.
But the fault lay not so much with the Americans as with the French officers
themselves, especially d'Estaing. The crews longed for action—anything but
this endless hanging around. Indeed, so bad were the relations between the two
"allies" that a violent riot broke out in Boston, in the course of which M. de
St-Sauveur, chief of the French staff of that town, was mortally wounded and
several French soldiers had bloody fights with American militiamen. Bougainville himself had no spark of affection for these sons of the New World. In a
letter in the possession of de Kérallain, he remarks on their pride, their caprices
and their puerilities, and on how amazed he was at their astonishment on first
glimpsing French soldiers, who they had been led by the British to believe were
all undersized. Speaking of the women, Bougainville wrote, "The American
women, virtuous or otherwise, have no liking for the French; so you can guess
how fond we are of them."

Bougainville was surprised one day by the arrival of the grandson of the
Iroquois chief by whom he had been adopted when he was campaigning in
Canada. Since that chief had considered himself the son of Bougainville, the
French commander now found himself the great-grandfather of the present
visitor!

The Comte d'Estaing finally left the unhospitable shores of America and
set sail for the West Indies, missing the British fleet as it emerged from New
York harbour. "I do not know", wrote Bougainville ruefully, "for what
manner of campaign the Toulon squadron is today prepared, as it is short of
tackle and has scant supplies. . . . *Ma foi*, I cannot conceive how the subsistence
of men can thus be put in danger, and for the hundredth time I repeat, God
alone knows how it will all end."

On 9 December the squadron dropped anchor off Martinique, where
Bougainville was greatly moved to see the *Boudeuse* "still proud and graceful in
the service of France". Most of the islands of the West Indies were then still
held by the British, and only Martinique, La Guadeloupe and St Lucia were
still in the hands of the French. But in August of the same year (1778), the Marquis de Bouillié, Governor of the French Windward Islands, wrested the island
of Dominica from the British, after a battle of extreme barbarity. The British
were about to take their revenge by an invasion of St Lucia. On 14 December,
d'Estaing, as soon as he was informed of the enemy operation, ordered his
squadron to proceed at once to the help of de Bouillié and appointed Bougainville to the reserve corps, composed of marines. "I belong", commented
Bougainville, "to the State, on land as well as at sea."

After a first encounter with the enemy, in which the *Guerrier* lost two men killed and three wounded, Bougainville succeeded in disembarking part of his troops. The enemy fire did great damage to the other French troops, who were deplorably short of ammunition, and, after repeated hesitations and useless manoeuvres, d'Estaing gave up any further attempt to capture the island. "Ah!" cried Bougainville, "what strength have our indecision and feeble and mistaken manoeuvres given to the English!" This engagement cost the French a thousand men, including some of their best troops.

The early months of 1779 were a period of relative inaction for the French fleet. To keep his men occupied, Bougainville arranged and supervised the making of blue tunics, white drill waistcoats and breeches for the sailors who were to take part in the landings, and whom he called his "amphibious militia". Without much trouble d'Estaing took possession of St Vincent, and the game of capturing and recapturing islands of the Antilles continued, without any results of importance. From time to time courtesies were exchanged between d'Estaing and Admiral Byron, the same whom Bougainville had encountered during his first voyage to the Straits of Magellan.

Reinforced by the squadron of de Grasse, Suffren and La Motte-Picquet, d'Estaing put to sea on 31 June with twenty-five ships. He captured Grenada and engaged Byron in a battle in which he was nearly victorious. The two squadrons, French and British, had reached the point of exhaustion before both disengaged. D'Estaing had already decided to return to France, but as he was a proud man he determined first to attempt some brilliant stroke, in order to return home a hero. Of what matter to him the shocking state of health of his men, so long as he could be crowned with a halo of glory? "The ambitious Vice-Admiral", noted Bougainville, "has been informed of the condition of his men and ships, but it seems that this was of no consequence to him. Of all evils which destroy poor human beings, the worst is to have their fate placed in the hands of an ambitious man."

In December of the preceding year, the British had occupied the town of Savannah, on the coast of Georgia. D'Estaing was determined to recapture it. On 1 September, the French troops were disembarked and camps pitched. Bougainville quickly noticed the total lack of organization. After six weeks of far from brilliant operations, the assault on the town began, but failed hopelessly, and the ambitious d'Estaing gained nothing from this mad venture except a wound in the leg.

Finally, in the early days of November, d'Estaing's squadron set out for France. As Bougainville watched the coasts of America recede, he expressed the bitterness with which he regarded this thoroughly useless campaign, cursing the whole enterprise on behalf of American emancipation. He had come to fear that the alliance that Louis XVI had concluded so readily with the insurgents was about to end in disaster for the French fleet. "The squadron", he wrote, "which might have destroyed Byron is dispersed, overwhelmed by sickness and misfortune, by hunger and thirst; and the troops raised for the defence of our colonies have been reduced to the merest handful." He continued his sombre warnings as to the future of the squadrons of de Grasse and La Motte-Picquet, which had remained in the Antilles.

On 15 December, Bougainville, exhausted and disillusioned, disembarked at Rochefort. As a reward for his services he was gazetted rear-admiral, but he felt unable to accept this promotion, since it specified that the new rear-admiral was to rank below another officer, the Marquis de Vaudreuil, younger than Bougainville and with very little experience of the sea. As mentioned earlier, Bougainville strongly disapproved of the preference given to "red" officers— that is to say, members of the aristocracy who had made the navy their career, and who referred contemptuously to any officer not of noble lineage as a "blue". Bougainville was of course considered a "blue".

In declining the promotion he wrote to the Minister of Marine,

> Were I named d'Estaing, Beauffremont or Rochechouart, I should yield, with all my heart, priority of rank to M. le Marquis de Vaudreuil, whom in all respects I regard as one of the best all-round officers the King has in his navy. But being born a commoner, I owe it to the class of useful men who enter the service in response to a vocation, not to condone by my consent the mortifications to which they are too often exposed. Without the slightest rancour, and without even a tinge of ill humour, I renounce even the rank of post captain. My position in this respect is all the more fortunate in that the sacrifice leaves me at the disposal of the service. I revert to the rank which the war procured for me in the land troops and which the King was good enough to allow me to retain.

By this letter Bougainville was forcibly protesting against the injustice of a system whereby promotion in the navy depended on the nobility or otherwise of one's birth. Cardinal Richelieu had attempted to have this iniquitous system abolished once and for all, but Colbert had revived it. (How different it was from the British system! Nelson was the son of a humble parson, and Captain Cook was a weaver's son and served his apprenticeship on a collier.) In response to his letter, Bougainville received permission to retire from the navy, but was accorded the rank of major-general in the land forces.

Chapter Three

Marriage—The Revolution—Old Age and Honours

Bougainville was now over fifty years of age, but he still looked and felt young. In 1780 he fell in love and married a lovely girl, twenty years his junior, who rejoiced in the charming name of Flore-Josèphe de Montendre. She was the daughter of a naval officer of high nobility who had been killed in action during the Seven Years War and was descended on her mother's side from one of the most pure and ancient families of Brittany. It was a completely happy marriage, but hardly was their honeymoon over when war broke out and Bougainville's presence was once more required.

Although now a lieutenant-general of the land forces, he was appointed to the command of the *Auguste*, a man o' war forming part of the squadron commanded by the Comte de Grasse, whom the Maréchal de Castries, Minister of Marine, had raised to the rank of lieutenant-general, with orders to carry help to the insurgents in America and to the forces in the Antilles. The Comte de Guichen had replaced d'Estaing, and in the year 1780 had carried out a brilliant campaign against Admiral Rodney. The ill health of de Guichen forced him to retire and it was de Grasse who took his place. Towards the end of August his squadron entered Chesapeake Bay, Virginia. The British General, Cornwallis, had taken up a postion on the coast, at Yorktown, with the object of keeping communications with the British army at New York clear. La Fayette, followed by Washington, set out to blockade Cornwallis, while de Grasse was to cut off all British communication by sea. Under the command of Admirals Hood and Graves, the British fleet appeared on the scene and immediately began an attack on de Grasse, who victoriously defeated them. This naval engagement proved the remarkable sense of naval strategy possessed by the French admiral. Cornwallis was obliged to capitulate, surrendering Yorktown and 7000 prisoners. During the course of the battle, the *Auguste* was in the van, and Bougainville so distinguished himself that de Grasse, in the presence of Washington, La Fayette and Rochambeau, commended him by saying, "the laurels of the engagement belong to you".

Bougainville next accompanied de Grasse to the Antilles, where, however, the French were less fortunate than in the Battle of Chesapeake Bay. In January 1782, de Grasse attempted to recapture the island of St Christopher from the

British, but failed disastrously and lost his advantage, never to regain it. Having
let slip the opportunity of annihilating Hood's squadron before Hood could
contact the fleet that Rodney was bringing from England, he could not prevent
the two British fleets from combining. In an attempt, with the help of the
Spanish fleet, to capture the island of Jamaica, he was closely followed by Rodney,
who on 12 April joined battle with him under the island fortress of Les Saintes,
to the south of La Guadeloupe. The subtle manoeuvres of Rodney disconcerted
the French fleet and deprived it of its best ships. De Grasse was taken prisoner.
Bougainville's ship was so badly damaged that he was quite unable to take as
active a part in the engagement as he or his commander would have desired.
Nevertheless, he accomplished the impossible and successfully rallied what
remained of the battered squadron. "The recollection of that fatal day . . . will
be ever present in my memory", he wrote.

This campaign of 1782 was a perpetual source of humiliation for Bougainville. His relations with de Grasse had come to be marked by constant bitterness,
and the admiral displayed towards him all the arrogance with which the "red"
officers were wont to disparage the "blues". Naturally Bougainville objected
to his admiral's aspersions—and sometimes did not fail to express, even in
public, his opinion of his chief's lack of capacity.

Bougainville returned to France more disillusioned than ever. Puns were
being made in Paris over the disaster of Les Saintes. "Without an act of Grace
[Grasse] we should have sung a Te Deum." The aged Duc de Richelieu, when
bestowing the command of the naval forces upon the Comte d'Estaing, wrote,
"Après avoir rendu grâce [Grasse] à dieu, il faut nous remettre un autre destin
[d'Estaing]" ("After having rendered thanks [Grasse] to God, we must now
put ourselves back in the hands of destiny [d'Estaing]"). And, as in France all
ends in song, satirical verses were composed concerning the unfortunate but
gallant admiral, whom the Americans had called "the intrepid Frenchman".
The brilliant victory at Chesapeake had been forgotten: only the defeat was
remembered.

On his return from captivity, de Grasse, the same who had praised Bougainville so highly for his performance at Chesapeake Bay, now laid the blame for
the defeat at Les Saintes on the commander of the *Auguste*, declaring that he
had not obeyed the orders signalled from the flagship. In 1784 a council was
held at Lorient to decide where responsibility for the defeat lay. Bougainville
defended himself with dignity and had no difficulty in proving that he had
never failed in his duty. His rigging and shrouds had been completely shot away
and he was in danger of losing his masts. In the circumstances he felt that all
that he could do was make for the island of St Eustace and there undergo
repairs. Nor did he judge it advisable to court certain and useless disaster by
leading his crippled squadron into the midst of the British fleet. His conduct was,
however, condemned; he was ordered to be publicly reprimanded; and he was
forbidden to attend Court for a time. De Grasse was acquitted by his judges,

probably because his captivity at the hands of the British was considered sufficient punishment, but he was nevertheless condemned by the King to exile at his château of Tilly.

The years passed. Both in Paris and on his property at La Brosse, near Villeneuve St Georges in the Val de Marne, Bougainville enjoyed a peaceful life with his delightful wife, who bore him three sons, whom he adored. But little by little the first rumblings of the Revolution were to be heard. Bougainville, soldier and sailor, could not remain inactive in face of the coming storm. He had been very well aware of the many injustices of the old regime and at the outset had been favourably disposed to liberal ideas, but in 1789, when the Bastille fell to the mob, he realized that the Revolution was to be no mere peaceful change of government, but that the whole country—indeed Europe—would be plunged into a blood-bath.

Just as in 1917 in Russia, it was the naval ratings who were the first to become intoxicated by the wave of liberty that was sweeping over the country. When one remembers that many were pressed into the service, that the conditions under which they had to serve were generally appalling, and that the majority of their officers were brutes, this is scarcely surprising. In Britain, conditions in the navy had not been much better, as was to be demonstrated by the "Mutiny of the Nore" in 1797. This outbreak of discontentment lasted from 20 May until 13 June, and was led by a seaman named John Parker, who styled himself "President of the Floating Republic". He was hanged from the yardarm of his ship and a few other men in the fleet were soon afterwards executed or flogged. In Brest in 1790, however, the mutiny assumed more serious proportions. The Comte Albert de Rions, who was in command there, found himself unable to repress the frenzy of the ratings and, unable to re-establish discipline, sent in his resignation. D'Estaing was considered for the post, but refused to leave Paris. The bourgeoisie of Brest were alarmed and clamoured for a leader who could succeed in moderating the unrestrained fury of the navy. For this task it was necessary that a man of universal popularity should be appointed. Bougainville was known throughout the fleet as a humanitarian officer, and, perhaps also because he was regarded as a "blue", the Government decided to create this lieutenant-general—"almost a rear-admiral", as he put it—Commander-in-Chief of the naval forces at Brest. On 30 November, he hoisted his flag on board the *Majestueux*. At the outset, Bougainville succeeded in re-establishing some order, but the revolutionary element soon got the upper hand. His orders were not obeyed; officers sent in their resignations. His position was hopeless. On 5 February 1791 he too tendered his resignation.

In September of the same year, the Minister of Marine, the Comte de Fleurier, resigned, and Louis XVI offered the post to Bougainville, but he refused it. In January 1792, the new Minister of Marine, the Marquis Bertrand de Molleville, realizing that in times of such grave crisis there was a paramount need for attaching to the Government men of Bougainville's qualities offered him the rank of vice-admiral, but, in view of the new regulations governing the navy, Bougainville felt obliged to refuse the appointment. He wrote to the Marquis de Molleville,

> Monsieur, I have received the letter with which you have honoured me. . . . Duty and honour both forbid me to accept an eminent rank, the duties of which are beyond my powers. Discipline—that all-sacred discipline, without which a navy above all cannot act—or rather, should I say, cannot exist—has been entirely subverted. A general officer can do nothing without able subordinates. In vain I seek for men who have combined theoretical knowledge of military tactics with actual combat experience. Such men have been very patient, but repeated and condoned insubordination has driven them all from the scene of their labours. Pray, Monsieur, be good enough to explain my feelings to the King, for I should be most unhappy were I unable to devote my declining days to the service of my country and be able to end my career as I began it. . . .

When on 20 June the infuriated mob forced its way into the Tuileries, Bougainville was at the King's side—ready to die in his defence. On 10 August he was there again, prepared to do anything to save the royal family of France. Then came the Terror, but Bougainville had no thought of emigrating. When the storm broke, he remained for a while on his property at La Brosse; then, as this was so close to Paris, he thought it wiser to leave with his family for La Becquetière, in the neighbourhood of Coutances. Although there were no outbreaks of bloody fury there, the local authorities, anxious to show their patriotic zeal, confined Bougainville to prison. The imprisonment was quite a family affair, for the doors of the gaol were freely opened to the wife and children of the great navigator.

In 1793, when the Terror was at its height, Bougainville concluded that his house at La Becquetière was no longer safe for his family. He therefore begged his wife to take their children and seek refuge in St Malo, at the house of Benjamin Dubois. Dubois, a shipowner, had been of great help to him when he was organizing his first expedition to the Falklands. Flore disguised herself in man's clothing and embarked for St Malo in a sloop, with her three children; but one of the sailors looked suspiciously at the beautiful passenger, whose disguise could hardly fail to conceal her sex. Suddenly approaching her, he said, "You are too pretty to be a man." For reply she gave him a resounding smack on the cheek; but the damage was already done. No sooner had she and her children arrived at St Malo than orders came from headquarters to send Bougainville to Paris—in other words to the scaffold. Fortunately, a few days later Robespierre fell and Bougainville was released.

Bougainville's old age brought him the honours he had never sought. In 1795 France recognized him at his proper value. The Directoire elected him a member of the Longitudinal Bureau and in the same year the doors of the Institut were opened to him.

In 1799 the Council of Five Hundred nominated him to compete with Barthélemy for the post of *directeur*, but it was Barthélemy who was elected. Nevertheless, Napoleon, who after his triumphant victories in Italy was the hero of all France, wished to make the acquaintance of the great navigator, and did so at a banquet given by Talleyrand. Bougainville was among the guests assembled there to salute the victorious young General, who singled him out and engaged him in long conversation. As a result of this interview, Bonaparte often consulted him with regard to his forthcoming expedition to Egypt. On his election as First Consul, Napoleon granted a pension of 40,000 francs to the old sailor, whom he jokingly referred to as "Monsieur le royaliste"—at which Bougainville was accustomed to smile, without making any denial. However, he had a great admiration, at the time, for the man who had dragged France out of the pit of anarchy. He was appointed a senator, and when Napoleon became Emperor was made Count of the Empire and Grand Officer of the Légion d'Honneur.

When the Emperor was looking for a successor to Decrés as Minister of Marine, he thought of bestowing the office on Bougainville. He sent for the old sailor, but when he came he remarked to him, "You are perhaps rather elderly for this post, Monsieur de Bougainville." To this Bougainville replied, "Sire, the aged Nestor was no less brilliant before Troy than the young Achilles, and Homer does not praise the one more than the other."

Despite this apt retort, Napoleon did not, after all, accord him the post.

Bougainville's last years were saddened by bereavements. He had acquired in 1799 a château and estate at Suisnes, in a picturesque corner of Brie, in the Île-de-France. There he devoted himself to the cultivation of roses. It was there in 1801 that his second son, Armand, was drowned before his mother's eyes. Armand was then sixteen years of age and was taking a swim in the river d'Yères when the fatal accident occurred—how or why remains a mystery. (Some writers claim that the scene was a pond on the estate, but this seems improbable.) The shock for Mme Bougainville was overwhelming, and she never recovered from it: on 7 August 1806, she died. Bougainville had by then sold his Suisnes estate and was living in Paris. His three remaining sons were a consolation and a pride to him. The eldest, Hyacinthe, who followed in his father's footsteps and joined the navy, was to become a rear-admiral. He, too, made voyages of exploration and visited Tahiti. Alphonse, the second surviving son, was an officer in the imperial armies, while the third, Adolphe, who went on to become a general of cavalry and serve in Spain, was a page to the Emperor.

In December 1808 Bougainville wrote to Adolphe,

> I have travelled four times on horseback along the route which you are about to follow; write to me and tell me if the road to the summit of Mont St Agnesi still passes through a vault cut through the rock. . . . In my days, the plateau on the summit was very often the graveyard of travellers. All the same, Biscay is a fine enough country; but I often observed the inhabitants and their animals sharing the same quarters.

"In my days"—these are the words of an old man; but his robust health did not forsake him. His mind was as active as ever and his truly French gaiety never altogether deserted him. His heart was ever generous and his actions were ever liberal. In the midst of universal respect and deep affection, Bougainville died on 31 August 1811, at the age of eighty-two, in his house in Paris. On 7 September his ashes were taken to the Panthéon. Inscribed on the pedestal of the urn were the words "Homage to the great men who deserve well of their country." His heart was placed at the foot of the tomb of his dear wife, in the cemetery of Montparnasse.

The Comte de Lacépède, President of the Senate, solemnly saluted the memory of his illustrious colleague, Count of the Empire, *membre, première classe* of the Institut and the Bureau des Longitudes, and, as the insignia placed on his coffin showed, Grand Officer of the Légion d'Honneur.

Notes

1. The post of Lieutenant de Police was created by Louis XIV. The holder of this office was responsible to the King for all merchandise bound for Paris; for supervising street cleaning and lighting; for combating fire and flood; and for ensuring the honesty of all transactions in Les Halles and other markets. In addition, any sort of violent crime, including rioting, fell within his jurisdiction.
2. The *mousquetaires noirs* and *gris*, so named after the colour of their horses. They were dragoon regiments.
3. Le Mercier, who had risen from the ranks to become a colonel, was among those later to be arraigned with Bigot for fraudulent misappropriation of government funds. Within a few years he had amassed a vast fortune by the sale of army property.
4. Lydius was a Dutch trader from Albany, suspected of being a spy in French pay. I can find no reference to a fort of that name. It was probably a fortified trading post.
5. This was not the experience of Wallis of the *Dolphin* when he put into Tahiti, where he stayed from 23 June to 27 July 1767. On arrival, such was the hostility of the natives that he was even obliged to open fire with cannon. Despite this unfortunate skirmish, Wallis soon established amicable relations with the natives. The introduction of venereal disease to Tahiti was attributed by the French to Wallis's men; by Wallis to the French.

Index

The index deals only with the essential matters connected with Bougainville and makes no attempt to cover less important people or events. The subheadings are placed in chronological order between the period 1729–1811. The initial B refers to Louis-Antoine de Bougainville throughout.